Easy Windows® 95
Second Edition

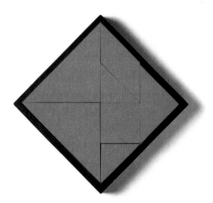

by Sue Plumley

Dedication

I dedicate this book to my nephew Hugh Bender, a bright and talented young man.

Credits

Publisher
Roland Elgey

Publishing Director
Lynn E. Zingraf

Editorial Services Director
Elizabeth Keaffaber

Managing Editor
Michael Cunningham

Director of Marketing
Lynn E. Zingraf

Acquisitions Editor
Martha O'Sullivan

Technical Specialist
Nadeem Muhammed

Product Development Specialist
John Gosney

Technical Editor
Keith Underdahl

Production Editor
Audra Gable

Book Designers
Barbara Kordesh
Ruth Harvey

Cover Designers
Dan Armstrong
Kim Scott

Production Team
Erin M. Danielson
DiMonique Ford
Trey Frank
Amy Gornik
Tony McDonald
Nicole Ruessler
Julie Searls

Indexer
CJ East

Composed in *Syntax* and *New Century Schoolbook* by Que Corporation

We'd Like to Hear from You!

As part of our continuing effort to produce books of the highest possible quality, Que would like to hear your comments. To stay competitive, we really want you, as a computer book reader and user, to let us know what you like or dislike most about this book or other Que products.

You can mail comments, ideas, or suggestions for improving future editions to the address below, or send us a fax at 317-581-4663. For the online inclined, Macmillan Computer Publishing has a forum on CompuServe (type **GO QUEBOOKS** at any prompt) through which our staff and authors are available for questions and comments. The address of our Internet site is **http://www.quecorp.com** (World Wide Web).

In addition to exploring our forum, please feel free to contact me personally to discuss your opinions of this book: I'm **104436,2300** on CompuServe, and I'm **jgosney@que.mcp.com** on the Internet.

Although we cannot provide general technical support, we're happy to help you resolve problems you encounter related to our books, disks, or other products. If you need such assistance, please contact our Tech Support department at 800-545-5914 ext. 3833.

To order other Que or Macmillan Computer Publishing books or products, please call our Customer Service department at 800-835-3202 ext. 666.

Thanks in advance—your comments will help us to continue publishing the best books available on computer topics in today's market.

John Gosney
Product Development Specialist
Que Corporation
201 West 103rd Street
Indianapolis, Indiana 46290
USA

About the Author

Sue Plumley has owned and operated her own business for eight years; Humble Opinions provides training, consulting, network installation, management, and maintenance to banking, education, medical, and industrial facilities. In addition, Sue has authored and coauthored more than 50 books for Que Corporation and its sister imprints, including the *10-Minute Guide to Lotus Notes 4*, *Special Edition Using Windows NT Workstation*, and *Easy Windows 95*. You can reach Sue via the Internet at **splumley@citynet.net** or on CompuServe at **76470,2526**.

Acknowledgments

A lot of people worked behind-the-scenes to help complete this book, and I'd like to thank everyone connected with it. Foremost, I'd like to thank Martha O'Sullivan, an excellent acquisitions editor because she's concerned about her authors and does everything she can to make our job easier. I appreciate her hard work, diligence, and friendship.

Thanks, too, to John Gosney for his guidance and advice. I want to thank Audra Gable for her hard work and perseverance; Audra always keeps me on my toes. Finally, thanks to Keith Underdahl, the technical editor, for checking the accuracy of the text.

Trademarks

All terms mentioned in this book that are known to be trademarks or service marks have been appropriately capitalized. Que Corporation cannot attest to the accuracy of this information. Use of a term in this book should not be regarded as affecting the validity of any trademark or service mark.

Contents

Part IV: Working with Folders and Files — 74

Part V: Printing with Windows — 104

Part VI: Personalizing Windows — 124

Contents

Part XI: References

212

Index

222

Introduction

Windows has always been an amazing graphical environment. Windows 95 advances utility and facility so that whether you're a beginning or advanced user, you can benefit from the new features, interface, networking capabilities, and so on. Using Windows 95, you can start and operate one or more applications easily and efficiently, as well as switch between applications effortlessly. In addition, you can share information between applications, customize the interface, manage and print files with ease, and perform many other tasks using the improved user interface and features.

Specifically, you can use Windows 95 to accomplish the following functions:

- **Manipulate windows.** Using the mouse, you can move a window around on the desktop (the background on which windows and icons appear) and resize any window. You can also arrange windows on the desktop, reduce or minimize a window, maximize a window, and so on. The control you have over the physical size and placement of the various windows enables you to work in your own way.

- **Manage files and folders.** Windows uses folders—representing directories—to hold files you use in your work. You can create new folders to hold files; you can open and close folders for viewing; and you can move, copy, rename, and delete folders to help organize your computer's directories and subdirectories. In addition, you can manage files by viewing them, sorting, copying, moving, renaming, and so on.

- **Use Windows' extensive Help features.** Windows provides an excellent Help feature that enables you to search for specific topics, view procedures, locate terms, and otherwise find the help you need to perform tasks in Windows. Windows also offers a handy shortcut feature that lets you quickly open documents, files, or folders by bypassing the menus and dialog boxes.

- **Control applications.** You can use both Windows and DOS programs within Windows, and you can start a program with Windows. You can also easily install new software applications and create folders to hold the programs.

- **Print from Windows.** Print documents from Windows applications, use the print queue to arrange printing priority, select and use a default printer, add other printers to the setup, change settings and options, pause and restart the print job, and more.

- **Control Windows fonts.** You can change the size and typeface of the Windows display fonts. Windows also enables you to insert symbols and other special characters into documents and other files. Additionally, you can use the Windows Font Manager to add and delete fonts, print samples of fonts, and so on.

- **Personalize Windows.** Windows provides the means to customize Windows features such as screen colors, mouse movements and speed, and passwords; it also enables you to easily change the system time and date.

- **Share information.** Windows enables you to easily switch between open programs so you can work in more than one file at a time. Furthermore, you can copy and move data in any application to another application and link data so that modified information is automatically updated from program to program.

- **Use Windows accessories.** Windows provides many *accessories*, or programs, you can use. For example, in addition to a word processor called WordPad, Windows offers a calendar, calculator, paint program, and several games for your amusement.

- **Maintain your system.** Use Wizards to notify Windows of newly installed hardware, to clean up your disk, and to scan disks for damage using ScanDisk.

Task Sections

The Task sections of this book include numbered steps that tell you how to accomplish such tasks as opening an application, arranging windows on the desktop, or writing and editing text in WordPad. The numbered steps walk you through a specific example so you can learn the task by actually doing it.

Big Screen

At the beginning of each task is a large screen that shows how the computer screen will look at some point during the procedure that follows in the task. For example, sometimes the screen shot shows the final result of the task, and sometimes it shows a feature (such as a shortcut menu) that's discussed later in the task.

"Why would I do this?"

Each task includes a brief explanation of how you might benefit from knowing how to accomplish the task.

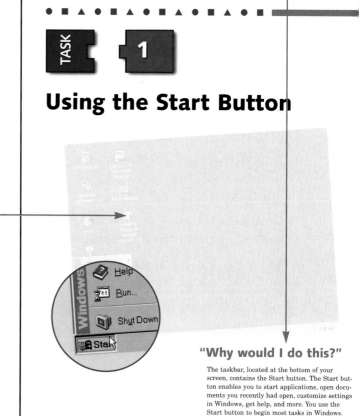

TASK 1

Using the Start Button

Windows

Help
Run...
Shut Down
Start

"Why would I do this?"

The taskbar, located at the bottom of your screen, contains the Start button. The Start button enables you to start applications, open documents you recently had open, customize settings in Windows, get help, and more. You use the Start button to begin most tasks in Windows.

8

Step-by-Step Screens

Each task includes a number of screen shots—one for each step of the procedure. The screen shots show how the computer screen looks at each step in the process.

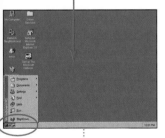

1 Point to the **Start** button on the taskbar with the mouse pointer. As you point to the button, a pop-up Help bubble briefly appears, saying Click here to begin. Go ahead and click—the Start menu appears.

Puzzled?

If you choose a command followed by an arrow (>),the program displays a secondary menu; if you choose a command followed by an ellipsis (...), the program displays a related dialog box.

Puzzled?

The Puzzled? notes explain areas in which you might have questions or need additional information. For example, a Puzzled? note might tell you how to undo a procedure (such as creating a folder) in case you decide you do not want to do it after all.

2 Move the mouse pointer to the **Programs** command to display a secondary menu of folders containing applications. For example, the Accessories folder contains Windows applications such as WordPad, Games, Calculator, and so on.

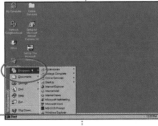

Missing Link

Your programs list may include many other folders that contain programs, such as Microsoft Office Applications, Lotus Applications, Microsoft Works, and so on.

Missing Link

Many tasks include short notes that tell you a little more about certain procedures. These notes define terms, explain other options, refer you to other sections when applicable, and so on.

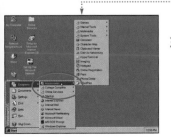

3 Point the mouse pointer at the **Accessories** folder to display a menu of programs in the folder. If you wanted to open one of the programs, you would point to the program name and click. For now, click on the desktop (anywhere outside the menus, but not on another icon) to close the Start menu. ∎

9

PART I

Controlling Windows

MICROSOFT NOW HAS TWO VERSIONS of Windows 95 in the marketplace. If you purchased Windows 95 software by itself, you have the original version. The only way you can get the second version of Windows 95 is pre-installed on a new PC. This upgrade to Windows can be supplied only by a computer manufacturer; therefore, you cannot install it yourself. The second version of Windows 95 offers a few features that work behind the scenes so the average user will not notice; those features are not covered in this book. The second version also employs an upgraded Internet Explorer and adds the Internet Mail and Internet News accessories, which are covered in this book. Other than a few cosmetic changes to the program, you won't notice a difference between the two versions of Windows 95. Therefore, I will not distinguish between the two versions in any way.

Using the Desktop and the Mouse

After you start Windows 95, you will see a screen called the desktop. From the desktop, you can open and switch between applications, search for specific folders, print documents, and perform other tasks. To effectively accomplish these tasks, you must know how to use a mouse; this section gives you a brief lesson in using the mouse.

The Desktop

Following is a list of items you'll see on your desktop when you first start Windows, along with a brief explanation of each:

- **The My Computer icon** opens into a window that contains icons representing your computer's drives and directories, the Control Panel, and the Printers folder. You will learn how to manipulate the My Computer window later in this part.

- **The Start button** provides a menu offering quick access to programs, documents, settings, Help topics, and so on.

- **The taskbar** is a horizontal bar located along the bottom of the screen that displays the Start menu and lists the open applications and documents.

- **Network Neighborhood** icon gives you access to all of the computers on the network, such as a file server containing shared folders (if you are connected to a network).

- **The Inbox** is a feature that enables you to send and receive faxes and e-mail messages through Microsoft Exchange.

- **The Microsoft Network** is an online service in which you can exchange messages with others; read news, sports, and weather; find technical information; and connect to the Internet.

- **The Internet icon** represents the Internet Explorer, a Windows program that enables you to attach to and explore Web pages on the Internet. In order to attach to the Internet, you must have a modem and a connection through an Internet Service Provider. For more information about ISPs and configuring your computer to access the Internet, see Part 9.

- **My Briefcase** is a handy tool you can use to transfer files from your hard drive to a floppy drive and back again. Using My Briefcase ensures that your files are up-to-date, no matter where you work on them.

- **You'll also see windows on the desktop**. Windows are rectangular areas containing folders, files, documents, dialog boxes, messages, and so on. You can easily move, size, and manipulate the windows to organize your desktop to suit your working routine. You open windows to view and make use of the items and applications within them.

The Mouse

You move the mouse on your desk until its corresponding on-screen pointer is pointing to the icon or other element you want to work with. *Pointing* to an element enables you to open, move, copy, delete, and otherwise manipulate the element.

You can press and release the left mouse button, called *clicking*, while you're pointing to an element. This action selects the element. In most cases, when I tell you to "click the mouse," you press the left mouse button. Sometimes, however, I might specify that you *right-click*, which means you should click the right mouse button instead of the left. When you point to an element and click the right button, you'll see a pop-up, or *shortcut*, menu from which you can choose a command.

If you click the mouse button and continue to hold the button down, you can move the mouse, and the selected item, across the desktop. This action is called *dragging*, or click and drag. You drag an item to move it to another location.

Finally, you will often be told to *double-click*. This means to press and release the left mouse button twice in quick succession. Double-clicking an icon or other item opens the item, activates a command, and so on.

When you finish working for the day, you must shut down Windows before you turn off your computer so you do not lose any unsaved data, files, or configuration. You'll learn how to shut down Windows later in this part.

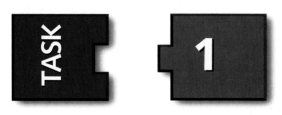
Using the Start Button

"Why would I do this?"

The taskbar, located at the bottom of your screen, contains the Start button. The Start button enables you to start applications, open documents you recently had open, customize settings in Windows, get help, and more. You use the Start button to begin most tasks in Windows.

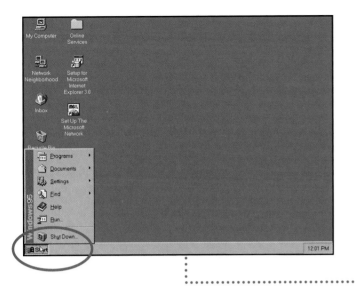

1 Point to the **Start** button on the taskbar with the mouse pointer. As you point to the button, a pop-up Help bubble briefly appears, saying Click here to begin. Go ahead and click—the Start menu appears.

Puzzled?

If you choose a command followed by an arrow (>),the program displays a secondary menu; if you choose a command followed by an ellipsis (...), the program displays a related dialog box.

2 Move the mouse pointer to the **Programs** command to display a secondary menu of folders containing applications. For example, the Accessories folder contains Windows applications such as WordPad, Games, Calculator, and so on.

Missing Link

Your programs list may include many other folders that contain programs, such as Microsoft Office Applications, Lotus Applications, Microsoft Works, and so on.

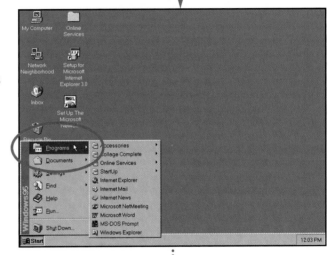

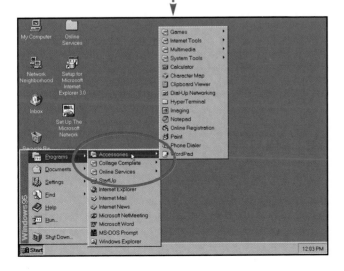

3 Point the mouse pointer at the **Accessories** folder to display a menu of programs in the folder. If you wanted to open one of the programs, you would point to the program name and click. For now, click on the desktop (anywhere outside the menus, but not on another icon) to close the Start menu. ■

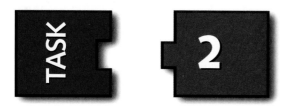

Opening a Window

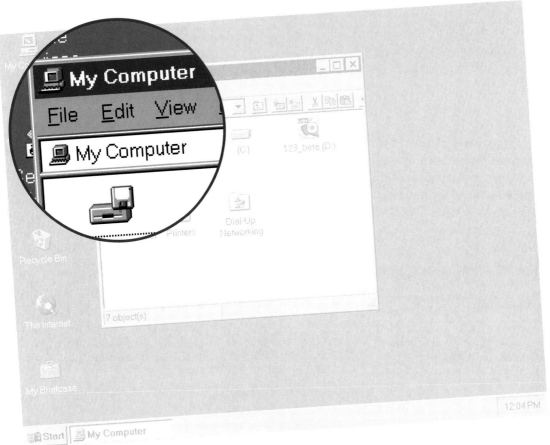

"Why would I do this?"

Windows 95 displays all of its information in on-screen boxes called windows. Before you can work with any of the information on your computer, you must know how to display (or open) these windows. Most windows are represented on-screen by small pictures called *icons*. You can open an icon and thus a window by double-clicking the icon, or you can use the alternative method described in this task.

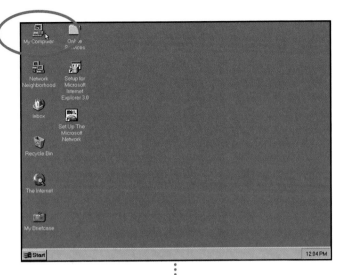

1 Point at the My Computer icon with the mouse pointer.

Missing Link

A shortcut for this two-step method of opening a window is to point to and double-click the icon. (If you have trouble getting your double-click timed just right, you can use the two-step method described here.)

2 Click the right mouse button to display the icon's pop-up, or shortcut, menu. Then click the word **Open** with the left mouse button to choose that command. The My Computer window opens.

Missing Link

Shortcut menus offer common commands related to the object you right-click. Try right-clicking on the taskbar and on the desktop to see the shortcut menus related to those items. To cancel a shortcut menu, click on the desktop with the left mouse button.

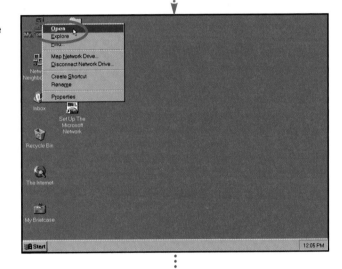

3 Note that a button for the My Computer window appears on the taskbar next to the Start button. ■

Missing Link

When you point the mouse at some buttons—and often at toolbars and other icons in Windows—a ToolTip appears. A *ToolTip* is a small box containing the name of the program or tool the button represents.

11

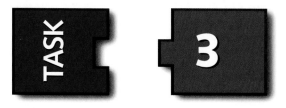

Reducing and Enlarging a Window

"Why would I do this?"

You can reduce (minimize) or enlarge (maximize) program and document windows to make your work easier. You might minimize a window to temporarily move it out of your way but keep it active for later use. On the other hand, you might maximize a window so you can see more of its contents on-screen.

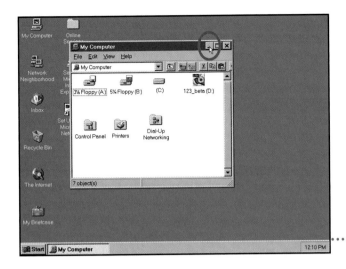

1 With the My Computer window open, point at the **Minimize** button—the button with an underline (_), located in the upper-right corner of the title bar—and click the left mouse button. The window disappears from the desktop and its button on the taskbar appears raised instead of recessed.

2 Point at the **My Computer** button on the taskbar and click the left mouse button. The My Computer window opens.

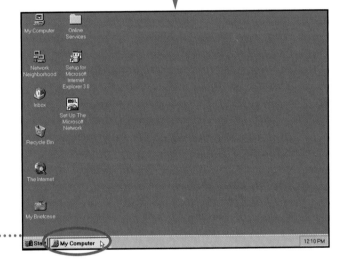

3 Point at the **Maximize** button—the button containing a rectangle, located in the upper-right corner of the My Computer window's title bar —and click the left mouse button. The window enlarges to fill the screen, and the Maximize button changes to the Restore button.

13

Task 3: Reducing and Enlarging a Window

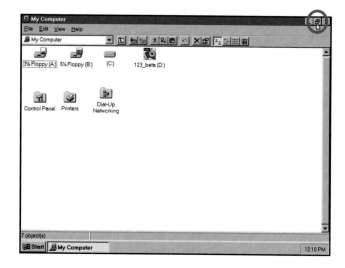

4 Click the **Restore** button—the one with two little overlapping boxes—to change the window back to its previous size. ■

Puzzled?

All application and document windows have Minimize, Maximize, and Restore buttons you can use to manipulate the size of the window.

Window Sizing Icons

Click This Icon	To Do This
▬	Reduce a window to a button on the taskbar.
▢	Enlarge a window so that it fills the entire screen.
⧉	Return a window to its normal size.

Moving and Resizing a Window

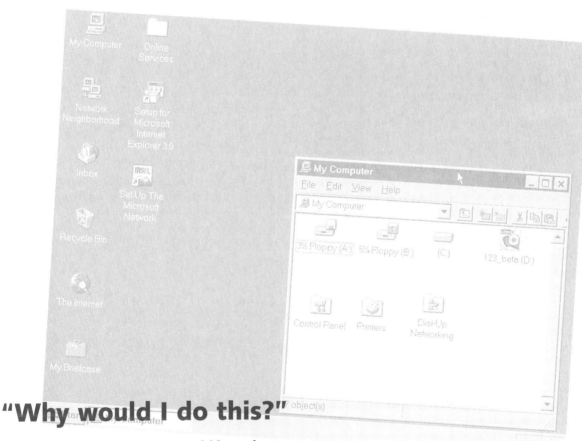

"Why would I do this?"

As you add more applications, folders, short-cuts, and so on to the desktop, you'll need more room to display these elements. You can resize a window to save room on the desktop, and you can move the windows around so you can see all the open windows at one time.

Task 4: Moving and Resizing a Window

1 To move an open window, point to its title bar, and then click and drag the window to a new position. The window border moves with the mouse pointer. When you release the mouse button, the window and its contents appear in the new location.

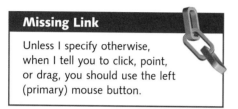

Missing Link

Unless I specify otherwise, when I tell you to click, point, or drag, you should use the left (primary) mouse button.

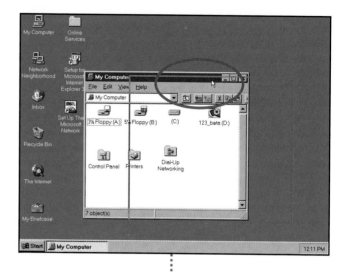

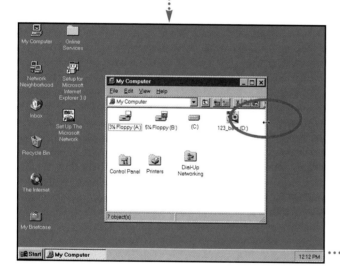

2 Position the mouse pointer over any window border until a double-headed arrow appears. Then drag toward the center of the window to reduce the size, or drag away from the center to enlarge the size. You can also drag a corner of the window to resize both dimensions proportionally at one time.

3 If a window is too small to show all of its contents, horizontal and vertical scroll bars appear. Click the arrow at either end of the scroll bar to move through the window to see its contents that are out of view. ■

Puzzled?

You can click anywhere in the scroll bar to jump in that direction to another part of the window; or you can point to one of the scroll arrows and hold down the mouse button to move in that direction more quickly.

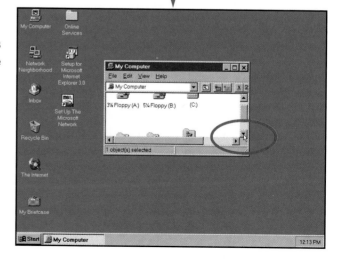

TASK 5

Using Menus

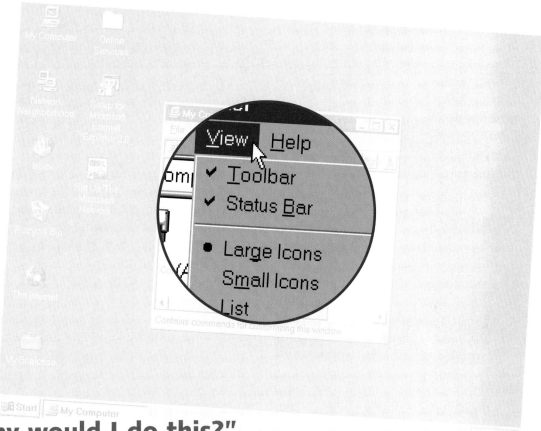

"Why would I do this?"

Although you can perform many tasks by clicking the mouse on different on-screen objects, you need to choose commands to perform the majority of Windows tasks. Commands are organized in menus to make them easy to find. In Task 2, "Opening a Window," for example, you displayed a shortcut menu from which you chose the Open command. Most windows contain menu bars across the top of the window that list the available menus; each menu then contains a group of related commands.

Task 5: Using Menus

1 Open the My Computer window. In the list of menus across the top of the window, point at and click the word **View**. The View menu opens.

Missing Link

The Control menu, located in the upper-left corner of the title bar, contains commands related to the open window, such as Restore, Move, Size, Close, and so on. You access the Control menu by clicking the icon at the left end of the title bar.

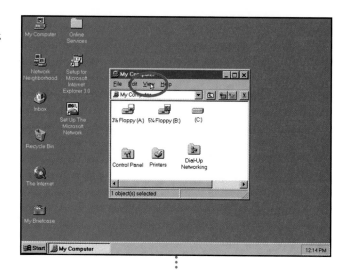

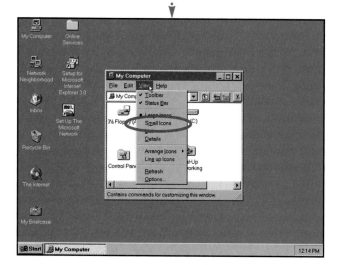

2 Click **Small Icons** to choose the command and close the menu. The icons in the My Computer window change to small icons. (To change them back, open the **View** menu and choose the **Large Icons** command.) ■

What You May See on a Menu	What It Means
Keyboard shortcut keys listed to the right of a command	You can press the shortcut keys instead of accessing the menu anytime you want to perform that command.
Check mark	The command is active. (More than one command on a menu can have a check next to it.)
A dot to the left of a command	The command has been selected. (Only one command in a menu can be selected at a time.)
An arrow to the right of a command	More options are available.
An ellipsis (...) after a command	A dialog box containing more options will appear if you choose that command.

Using Shortcut Menus

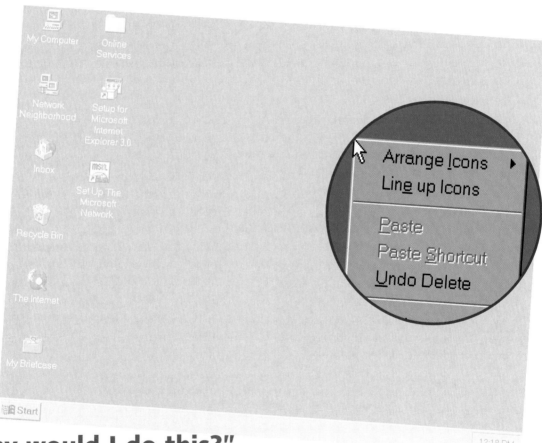

"Why would I do this?"

Shortcut menus, also called quick menus and pop-up menus, provide common commands related to the selected item. You can, for example, quickly copy and paste, create a new folder, move a file, or rearrange icons using a shortcut menu. Shortcut menus can contain the same symbols as regular menus to indicate a secondary menu, dialog box, and so on.

Task 6: Using Shortcut Menus

1 Point to any blank place on the desktop and right-click. A shortcut menu appears.

Missing Link

Make a habit of right-clicking in any new window you open and on any new icon you see to discover new menus and commands. Different shortcut menus appear depending on what you're pointing to when you right-click the mouse.

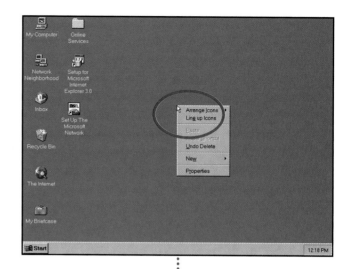

2 Click the **Arrange Icons** command. In the secondary menu that appears, click the **AutoArrange** command. Windows rearranges the icons on the desktop, placing them in a straight line. Notice too, that if you go back to the shortcut menu, the Auto Arrange command has a check mark beside it; this means that no matter where you move an icon on the desktop, it will revert back to its original position because the Auto Arrange feature is activated.

3 Right-click the desktop, choose **Arrange Icons**, and click the **Auto Arrange** command again. This removes the check mark and deactivates the command so you can freely move your icons around on the desktop. ■

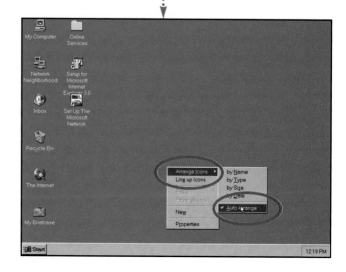

TASK 7

Changing the Windows Display

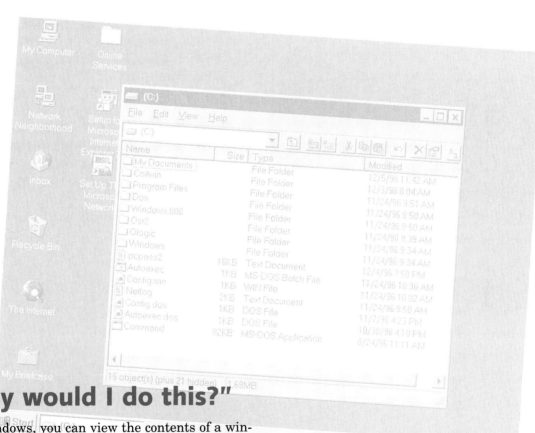

"Why would I do this?"

In Windows, you can view the contents of a window in a variety of ways. By default, Windows uses large icons to display the contents of a window. If you want to see more of a window's contents at one time, you can change the view to small icons (as you learned in the previous task). You can also display such details about an item as its type, its size, and the date it was last modified. (Then you could even sort the contents of the window by those details.) Changing the way a window displays its contents can make it easier to find what you need.

1 In the My Computer window, open your hard drive by double-clicking its icon (usually C:). Open the **View** menu and click the **Details** command. The window now displays elements in list form. (You may need to enlarge the window to see all the file details.)

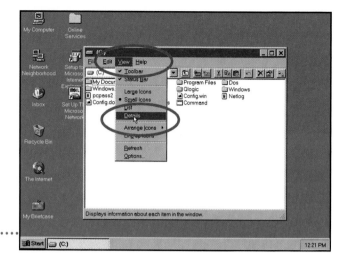

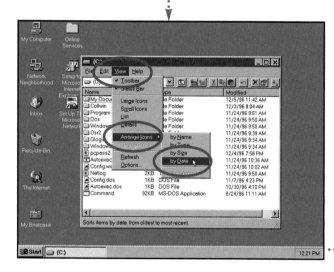

2 Open the **View** menu again and choose **Arrange Icons**. In the secondary menu that appears, choose **By Date**. Windows rearranges the folders and files in the window according to the date they were last modified.

3 To change back to the original view, open the **View** menu and click the **List** command. You can resize the window if necessary. ■

Puzzled?

You can rearrange the icons in the window by dragging each one to a new location. If the icons will not move, open the **View** menu and click the **Arrange Icons** command to remove the check mark.

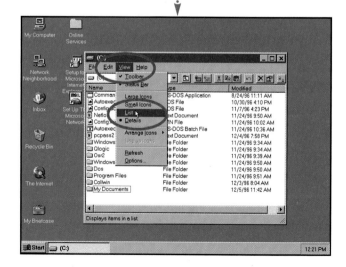

Arranging Windows on the Desktop

"Why would I do this?"

As you work, you will often have several windows open on the desktop at one time. The windows probably overlap each other, which can make it difficult to find what you want. To make your work easier and more efficient, Windows enables you to arrange the windows on the desktop in several different ways.

Task 8: Arranging Windows on the Desktop

1 Open multiple windows on the desktop. Then point to a blank area on the taskbar and right-click to reveal the shortcut menu.

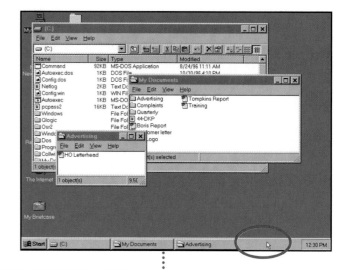

Puzzled?

If you have trouble finding an unoccupied space on the taskbar, you can enlarge the bar in the same way you enlarge a window. To enlarge the taskbar, position the mouse pointer on the bar's border until you see a double-headed arrow; then drag the border upward to enlarge the bar.

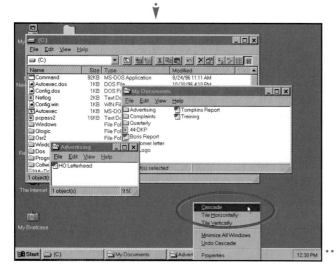

2 From the shortcut menu, choose **Cascade** to display the windows in an orderly fashion. Windows arranges the open windows so they overlap and resizes them so they are all the same size. To work in any of the open windows, click the mouse in that window to make it active. The active window moves to the front of the stack, and its title bar is a different color

3 To display all open windows in equal sizes, right-click the taskbar and choose **Tile Horizontally** or **Tile Vertically.** ■

Missing Link

After you rearrange multiple open windows, you can resize a window or move it as described in Task 4, "Moving and Resizing a Window."

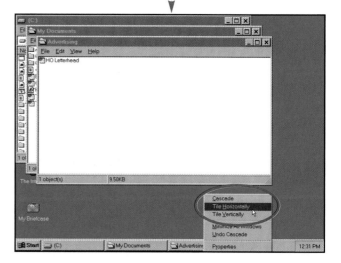

Closing a Window

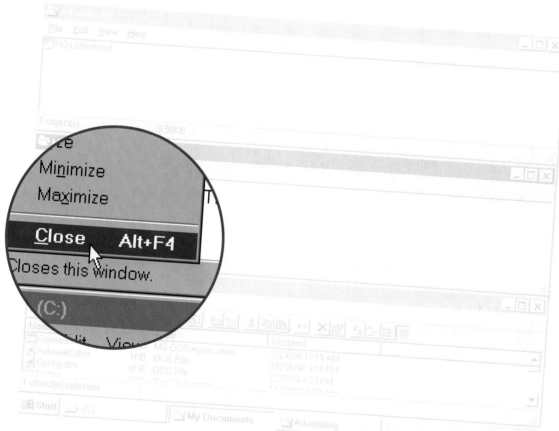

"Why would I do this?"

You close a window when you are finished working with it and its contents. Too many open windows clutter the desktop as well as the taskbar. This task shows you various methods of closing windows.

Task 9: Closing a Window

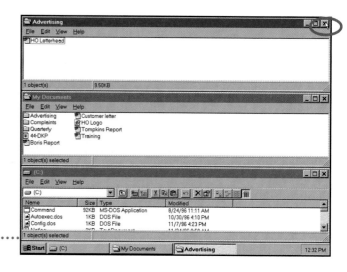

1 You can close a window by clicking the **Close** (X) button in the upper-right corner of the window's title bar.

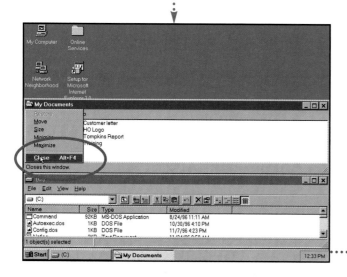

2 Another way to close a window is to click the **Control-menu** box in the upper-left corner of the title bar and choose **Close** from the Control menu. (When you click the Control-menu box, Windows displays the Control menu, which contains commands for controlling the active window.)

3 You can also close a window by selecting the window, opening the **File** menu, and then choosing the **Close** command. ■

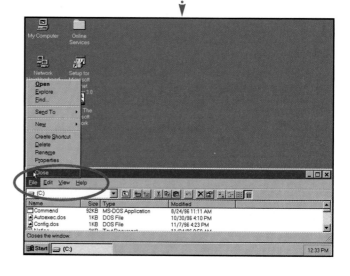

Missing Link

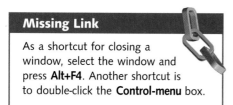

As a shortcut for closing a window, select the window and press **Alt+F4**. Another shortcut is to double-click the **Control-menu** box.

Using a Dialog Box

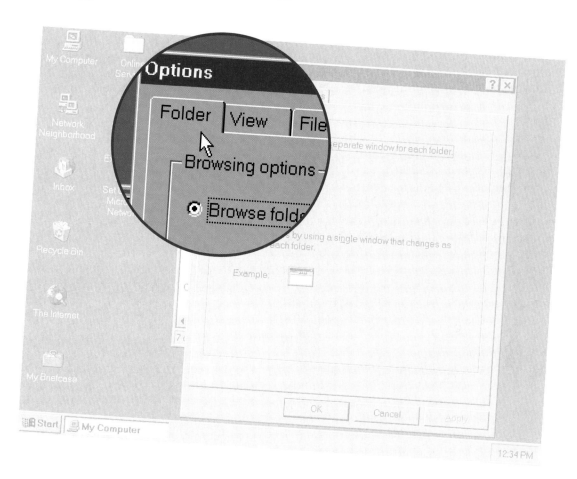

"Why would I do this?"

Dialog boxes contain options from which you
can choose in order to control windows, applications, document formatting, and a host of other
procedures. Dialog boxes are used throughout
Windows; luckily, all dialog boxes have common
elements and all are treated in a similar way.
This task shows you how to open and maneuver
a dialog box.

Task 10: Using a Dialog Box

1 In the My Computer window, select the **View** menu and choose **Options**. (Remember, selecting a command with an ellipsis following it displays a dialog box containing more related options.)

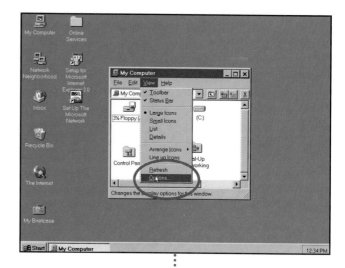

Missing Link

When a dialog box is open, you cannot perform any other action until you either accept changes by choosing OK or cancel the dialog box. You can also press **Enter** to accept or press **Esc** cancel the box.

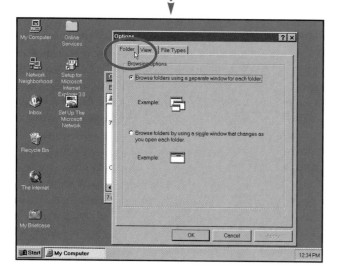

2 The Options dialog box appears. This particular dialog box contains three tabs which hold information and options relating to viewing windows. To view a tab's contents, click the tab (such as Folder or View). ■

Puzzled?

There is a difference between option buttons and check boxes. Option buttons are round white buttons that contain a black dot when selected. You choose only one option button in a group. (Choosing a second option deselects the first.) Check boxes are square boxes that *indicate* options (not option buttons!) that you can choose from. Select the option by clicking the box, and a check mark appears in the box. You can check one or more check boxes in a group.

Shutting Down the Computer

"Why would I do this?"

If you turn off the power to your computer
before you properly shut down the computer,
you could lose valuable data or damage an
open file. Windows provides a safe Shut Down
feature that checks for open programs and
files, warns you to save unsaved files, and
/prepares the program for you to turn off your
computer. You should always shut down before
you turn off the power.

1 Before shutting down the computer, close all open programs. You might also want to close open windows and folders, but that is not necessary.

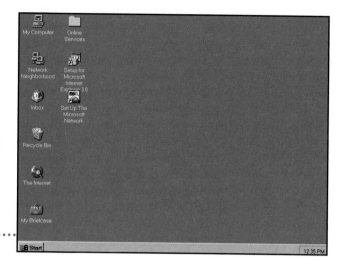

2 Open the **Start** menu and click **Shut Down**. Windows checks the system and prepares for the shut down, and displays the Shut Down Windows dialog box.

Missing Link

Often, you need to work from DOS instead of Windows. Windows 95 provides an easy way to boot to DOS. When you choose Shut Down, the Shut Down Windows dialog box appears. From the Are You Sure You Want To list, choose the **Restart the Computer in MS-DOS Mode** option and then choose **Yes**.

3 The default selection in the Shut Down Windows dialog box is Shut Down the Computer? Click **Yes** to complete the task. Windows displays a final screen that tells you when it is safe to turn off the power to your computer. ■

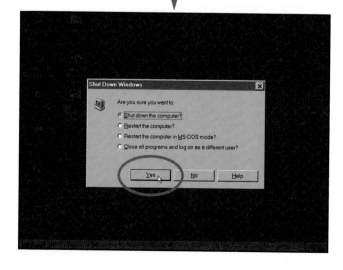

PART II

Getting Help

Windows provides various Help features to help you perform complex and everyday tasks such as using icons, inserting information, installing hardware and software, locating files, using the mouse, moving files, and so on.

When you initiate the Help feature from the Start menu, the Help window appears. The Help window contains three tabs, which provide you with three different ways to find the information you want: Contents, Index, and Find.

- **Contents** lists general topics such as Introducing Windows, Tour: Ten minutes to using Windows, How To…, and so on.

- **Index** lists all Help topics. To use it, you enter a topic, and the index moves to that Help entry.

- **Find** offers a text box in which you type a word you want to find; then a list of related topics appears.

When you choose a topic, Help displays a window describing how to perform the task or use the feature step-by-step. Help windows are like any other window; they include borders, Minimize and Maximize buttons, a Control-menu box, and so on. You can move, resize, and close Help windows just as you do any other. Refer to Part 1 if you need instructions on how to manipulate windows.

Included in many of the Help topics are shortcuts that lead directly to a dialog box or application. For example, in the Help window explaining how to use the Briefcase, one step offers a "click here" shortcut that enables you to create a Briefcase for immediate use.

In conjunction with the Help feature, you can add *annotations*, or notes, to any Help window to remind you of information that might be helpful the next time you access the topic. When you add an annotation, Windows displays a paper clip beside the topic in the topic's window. All you have to do is click the paper clip, and Windows displays your comments. Another handy benefit of the Help feature is that you can print any Help topic for easy reference.

In addition to the Help topics, Windows includes other forms of assistance. ToolTips are handy pop-up boxes that describe tools and buttons within the program. They appear when you point at a tool with the mouse pointer. Windows also provides a context-sensitive tool called What's This?, which appears as a question mark button in dialog boxes. To use it, you click the question mark, and then you can click any item in the dialog box for descriptions and definitions of that item or option.

Starting Help

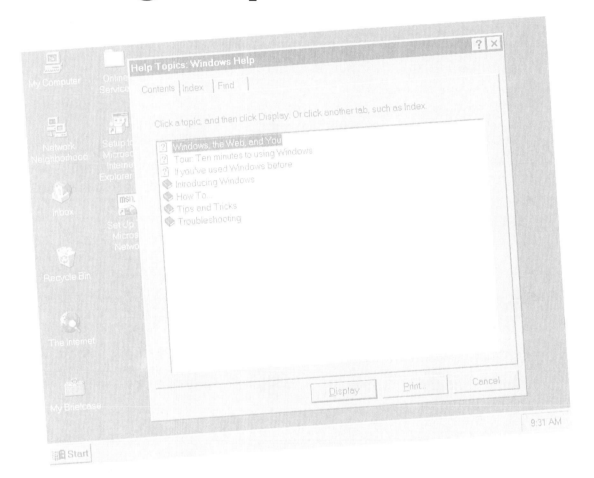

"Why would I do this?"

Whether you are a new or experienced Windows user, you will need help at some point with a procedure or task, such as setting up a printer, finding a document, or linking between applications. The newest version of Windows makes it easy and convenient to find that help. This task shows you how to start the Help features.

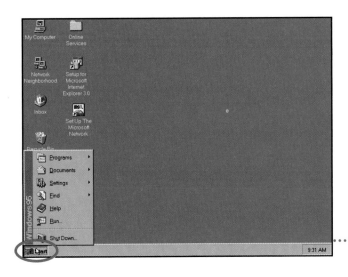

1 Click the **Start** button on the taskbar to display the Start menu.

2 From the Start menu, choose **Help**. The Help window appears. You can take a ten-minute tour of Windows by clicking the **Tour...** option in the Contents tab.

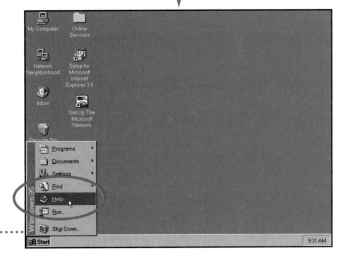

3 The Help Topics window includes three tabs (Contents, Index, and Find) from which you can choose. Each one provides a different type of assistance; click the tab you want to use. Tasks 13, 14, and 15 cover the use of these three tabs in detail. There you'll learn how to find help for any questions you have. ■

TASK

13

Finding Specific Help

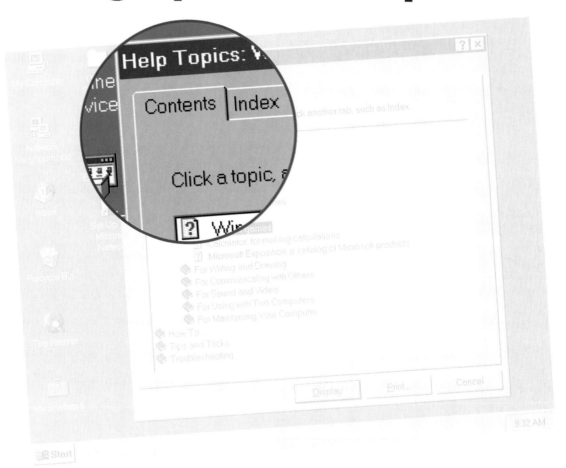

"Why would I do this?"

Use the Contents tab of the Help window to locate help for performing specific procedures, such as printing a document or installing new software. The specific topics included in the Contents tab quickly refer you to everyday tasks you might need to perform in the program.

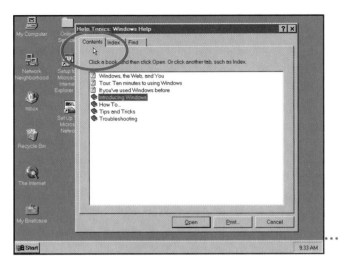

1 Start the Help program as explained in the previous task. In the Help Topics window, click the **Contents** tab if it is not already showing. (The last tab you viewed is the one that appears when you open the Help window.)

2 To view subtopics under any subject in the Contents tab (for example, How To…), click the book icon beside the topic. The topic becomes highlighted (white text on a black background). Then click the **Open** button at the bottom of the window to open the list of subtopics. The book opens, and a list of subtopics appears. Alternatively, you can double-click the book to open it.

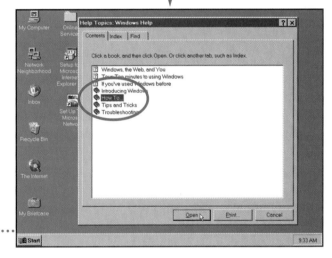

3 In the list of How To topics, double-click the topic **Print**. The book opens, and a list of related topics appears.

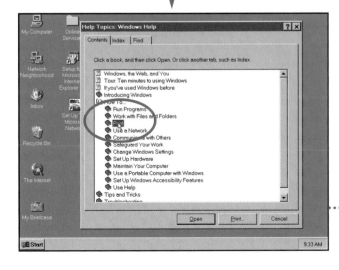

Missing Link

You can double-click an open book icon at any time to hide the subtopics listed below that topic. You also can choose any topic icon and click the **Print** button to print a hard copy of the topic.

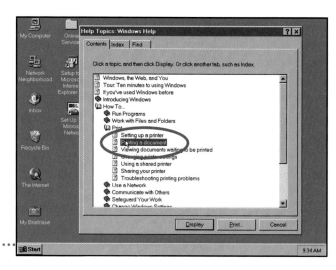

4 Double-click any one of the topics for more information. The Help Topics window (the main window) minimizes, and the topic window (a secondary window) appears. When you minimize the Help Topic window, it appears as a button on the taskbar.

5 After viewing the Help topic, click the **Help Topics** button to return to the Help Topic window and the Contents list. The specific topic window remains open in the background; when you choose another topic, the main Help window minimizes and the topic's procedure appears in the secondary topic window. ■

Puzzled?

Help's secondary topic windows stay on top of all other windows (except Help's main topic window) so you can use the step-by-step procedures as you work. If you close the secondary menu, you close Help, thus removing the icon from the taskbar. Therefore, you should minimize the secondary window if you want to use Help again later.

Locating a Topic

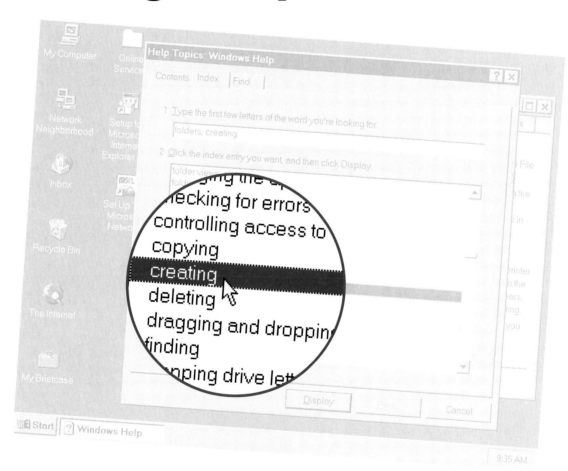

"Why would I do this?"

If you want to find help on a specific topic, such as storing files by size or editing text, use the Index tab in the Help Topics window. Topics listed in the index are in alphabetical order. In addition, the Index lists many more topics than does the Contents tab of the Help Topics window. This task illustrates how to use the Index in the Help Topics window.

1 Start Help as explained in Task 12. In the Help Topics window, choose the **Index** tab by clicking it (if it is not already showing). A list of indexed Help topics appears.

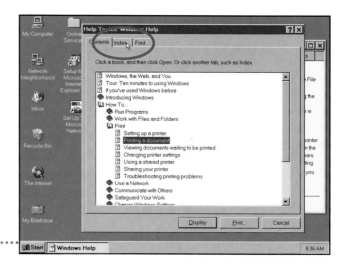

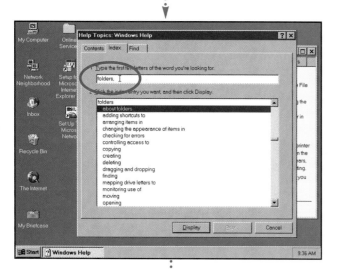

2 A blinking cursor appears in the text box at the top of the tab. Enter the name of the topic for which you want to search; in this case, type **folders**. As you type, the list jumps to the topic for which you are searching.

Missing Link

You can alternatively scroll through the list of topics on the Index tab; however, scrolling through the entire list takes a long time.

3 Double-click the word **creating** in the list of subtopics under "folders." If that subtopic does not contain any further subtopics, a secondary topic window appears, displaying step-by-step instructions for creating a folder. However, if the subtopic you choose offers more than one available topic, the Topics Found window appears. Choose the appropriate topic by double-clicking it, and then the secondary topic window appears. ■

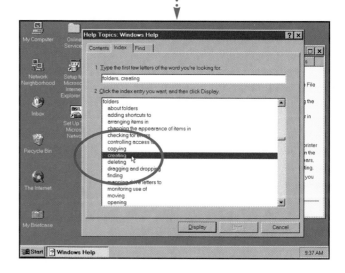

Using the Find Feature

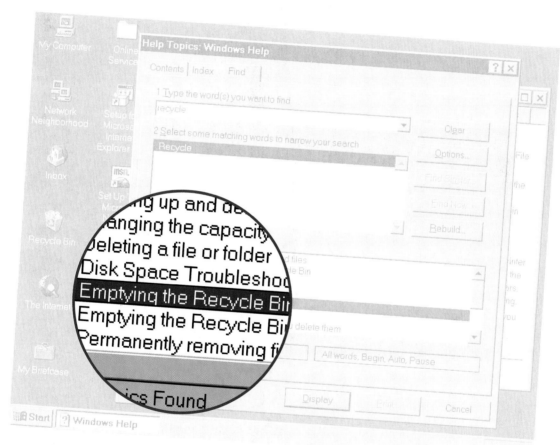

"Why would I do this?"

The Windows Help Topic called Find enables you to search for specific words within the Help topics. Before you can use the Find feature, you must enable Windows to compile the Find list. To do so, you choose the Find tab in the Help Topics window. You create the list only once by following the directions on-screen; from that point on, the Find list is available in the Help Topics window.

Task 15: Using the Find Feature

1 To view the Find list, open the **Start** menu and choose the **Help** command. The Help Topics window appears. You can use the Find tab to search for help on formatting disks, memory troubleshooting, saving a file, setting up a printer, and a multitude of other procedures in Windows.

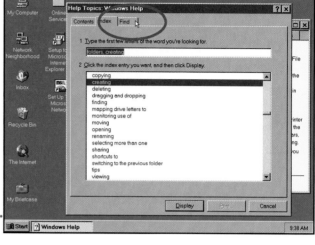

2 Choose the **Find** tab. If you have not used the Find tab before, Windows prompts you to set up the Find list. Follow the directions on-screen. It may take a few minutes to index all of the Help topics; when Windows finishes, the Find tab appears again.

Puzzled?

If you aren't sure which type of help to use, try all three of them; after using each a few times, you'll decide what works best for you.

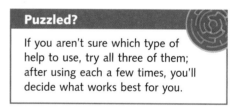

3 Enter the word or words you want to find in the 1 Type the Word(s)... text box. For example, type **recycle**. As you type, Windows jumps to a matching word or words in the second area (2 Select Some Matching Words to Narrow Your Search) and in the third area (3 Click a Topic). In the bottom list box, click the topic you want—for example, **Emptying the Recycle Bin**—and then click the **Display** button. The Help Topic secondary window appears with directions on how to empty the Recycle Bin.

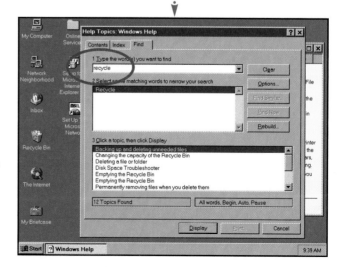

4 To read the definition of any underlined word or words in a Help window, position the mouse pointer over the word; the pointer changes to a hand. Click the mouse, and a definition appears.

Puzzled?

There are two Emptying the Recycle Bin Help Topics. The first tells you how to empty the bin, and the second offers information about viewing the contents of the bin and freeing disk space.

5 Click anywhere to close the definition box. Often secondary Help boxes have a button for related subjects at the end of the text; you can click that button to find more help on the topic. Choose **Help Topics** to return to the Find tab.

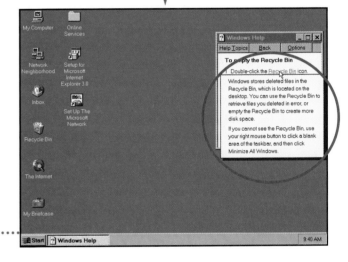

6 To close the Help Topics window, click **Cancel**. The secondary Help window remains open; if you want to close the secondary box, click the **Close** (X) button. ■

TASK 16

Adding Notes to a Help Topic

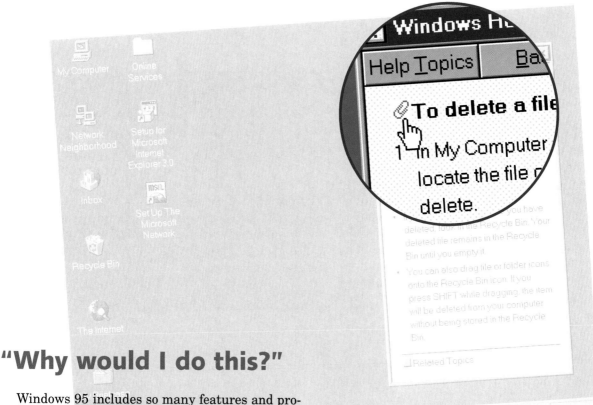

"Why would I do this?"

Windows 95 includes so many features and procedures that you may often need help completing tasks you don't do everyday. Help offers a way you can add notes or comments to Help topics for future reference. When you've added an annotation, or note, to a Help topic, Windows displays a paper clip in the dialog box to remind you of the note the next time you access that Help topic. You click the paper clip to display the annotation.

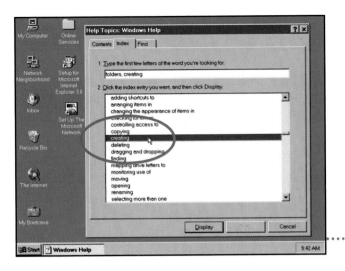

1 Open the Help window and choose the **Index** tab. In the first text box, type **folders**, and then double-click **creating**. The Topics Found window appears. From the list of topics, choose **Creating a Folder** and click **Display**. The secondary Help window appears.

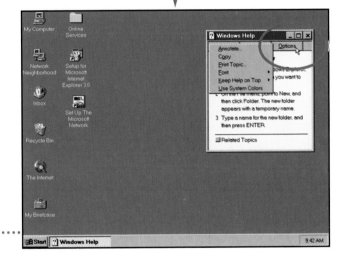

2 In the secondary Help window, click the Options button to display the Options menu; choose Annotate. Notice with this menu, you can also choose to print the topic, change the font size, copy the topic, and change system colors.

3 Enter the text in the **Current Annotation** text box and choose **Save**. A small paper clip appears beside the subject in the secondary Help window. To view or edit the annotation, click the paper clip. ■

Printing Help

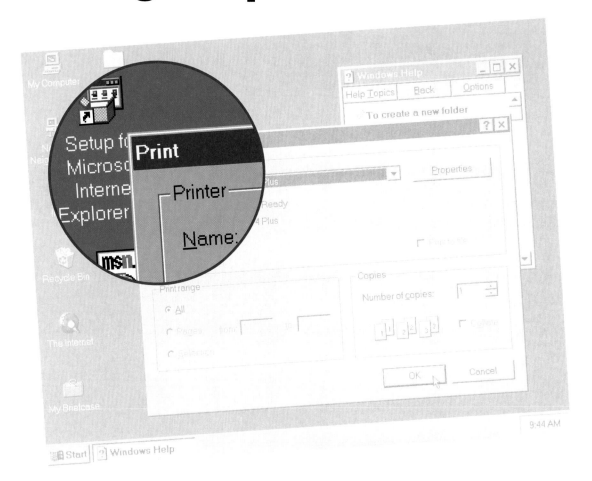

"Why would I do this?"

Although you can read instructions from a secondary Help window and the window stays on top of other windows while you work, it's often easier to print a Help topic for future reference. You can choose a topic in the Help window and print it quickly and easily. Part 5, "Printing with Windows," explains the finer points of printing.

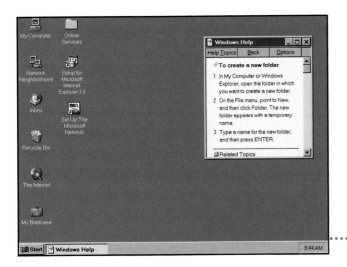

1 Display the secondary Help topics window by selecting a topic in the Index, Find, or Contents tab of the Help window.

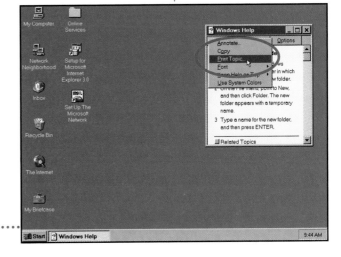

2 In the secondary Help topics window, choose the **Options** button, and then select **Print Topic** from the menu that appears. (Remember that an ellipsis after the menu command means a dialog box containing related options will appear.) The Print dialog box appears.

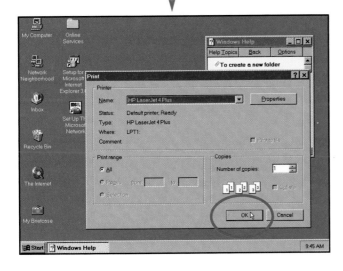

3 Choose the printer, number of copies, and print range. Then click **OK** in the Print dialog box to print the Help topic. ■

Using Context-Sensitive Help

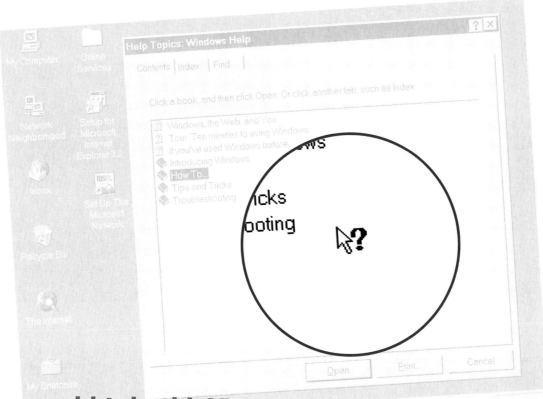

"Why would I do this?"

In many windows and dialog boxes, Windows
includes an additional Help feature called
What's This?, which is represented by a question mark in a window's title bar. You can use
this Help feature to get help on specific options
or items in a dialog box. This task describes
how to use the What's This? feature.

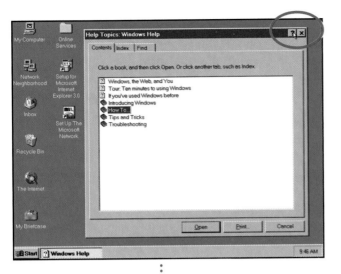

1 To use the context-sensitive What's This? feature, click the question mark (**?**) button in the title bar of any window or dialog box. For example, click the question mark button in the Help Topics main window. The mouse pointer changes to a pointer connected to a large question mark.

Puzzled?

If a dialog box does not contain the What's This? question mark, try pressing the **F1** button for help.

2 Move the pointer to any part of the dialog box about which you have a question. Click the left mouse button, and a box appears with an explanation or definition.

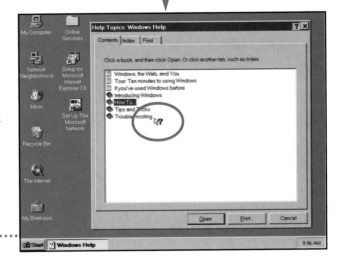

3 After reading the explanation, click anywhere within the Help box to close the context-sensitive box. Close the Help Topics window by clicking the **Close** (X) button in the title bar. ■

PART III

Using Applications in Windows 95

ONE ADVANTAGE TO USING WINDOWS is the enormous quantity of Windows applications available. Various companies produce word processing, database, spreadsheet, drawing, and other programs you can use in Windows. Such a variety of applications provides you with all the tools you need to perform your everyday tasks.

Windows applications are easy to open and use. Using the Start menu, you simply select the application from the Programs list, and it opens. You can also start a program from the My Computer or Explorer window, both of which give you quick access to any document or program.

Each open application appears in its own window, and you can minimize, maximize, resize, move, and rearrange application windows on the desktop (as you learned in Part 1). As you may remember, taskbar buttons represent minimized applications, giving you quick and easy access to the program and allowing for smooth switching between the open programs.

You can create documents, spreadsheets, or other data in Windows applications and save that information for later use. Windows enables you to save data in files of different names and in various locations on your hard disk or a floppy disk. You can open a file at any time to view, edit, or print it.

In addition, you can create shortcuts representing applications and place those shortcuts on the desktop. Using a shortcut makes accessing the application faster and easier. You can also delete a shortcut when you no longer need it.

Windows comes with several accessory programs (a word processor, paint program, calendar, calculator, and so on) that you can open and use while working in Windows. Additional Windows applications are easily installed as well. Other applications designed for use with Windows behave the same as Windows accessories; for example, you open, close, manipulate windows, and so on, the same in Word for Windows as you do in the WordPad accessory.

You can also open and use DOS programs (such as WordPerfect for DOS or Lotus 1-2-3 for DOS) within Windows. However, it is important for you to realize that opening and using large files from DOS programs within Windows may take extra RAM to work efficiently. See Part 11, "References," for more information about using DOS programs with Windows 95.

Starting an Application with the Start Menu

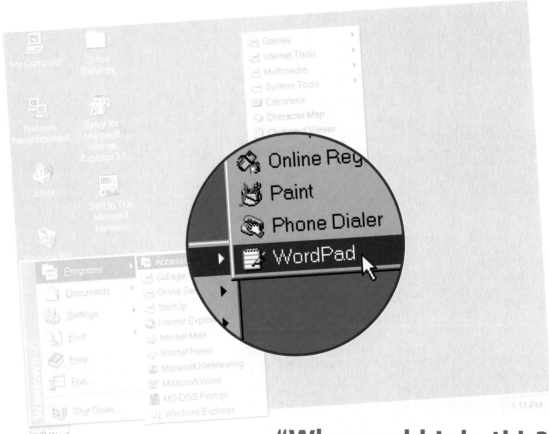

"Why would I do this?"

When you install a Windows application, the program's installation procedure creates an application folder that Windows places on the Start menu. You can open the folder and start the program through the Start menu. Whether the application is a Windows accessory, word processor, database, spreadsheet, or other program, it's easy to open and use in Windows.

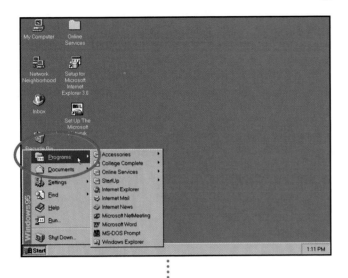

1 Open the **Start** menu and choose the **Programs** command. The Program menu appears.

Missing Link

You also can open an application by choosing **Start**, **Documents** and selecting any of the listed documents. The documents in this menu are those you've most recently opened. When you select the document you want to open, the application automatically opens as well.

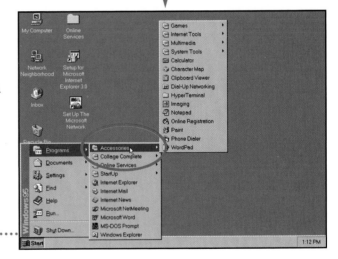

2 On the Programs menu, select the program group that contains the application you want to start. The folder's contents appear on a secondary menu.

3 Click the application you want to start, and the application opens in its own window. ■

Starting an Application from a File

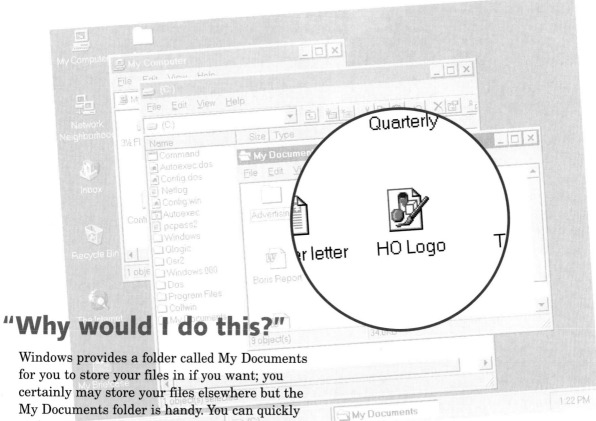

"Why would I do this?"

Windows provides a folder called My Documents
for you to store your files in if you want; you
certainly may store your files elsewhere but the
My Documents folder is handy. You can quickly
and easily open any application by going to the
My Documents folder and double-clicking a file
created in that application. You also can open
the application by double-clicking a file in the
Explorer. The Explorer (which is similar to the
File Manager in Windows 3.x) provides another
way of viewing folders (directories), subfolders
(subdirectories), and files in Windows 95.

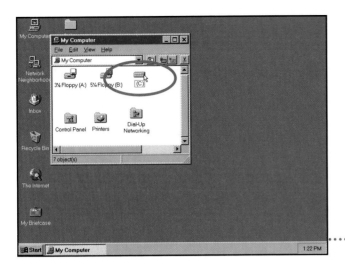

1 Open the **My Computer** window, and then double-click the icon for your hard drive to open another window showing the hard drive's contents. (Your contents list may look different from that in the figure.)

2 Open the **My Documents** folder to display all documents you've saved there.

Missing Link

You can create new documents in the My Document window. Choose **File**, **New** and select an application to use to create the document. The applications listed are the programs you've added to your Windows 95 setup. The Windows accessories (WordPad and Paint, for example) are not listed; however, you can save documents created in the accessories applications in the My Documents folder.

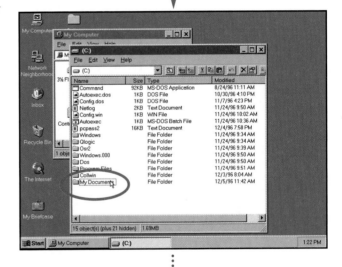

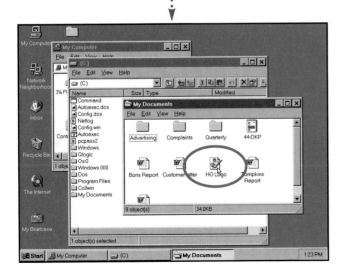

3 Double-click any file created in an application on your machine. The application opens and displays the file, so you can work on it or print it. ■

TASK **21**

Opening a File with the Explorer

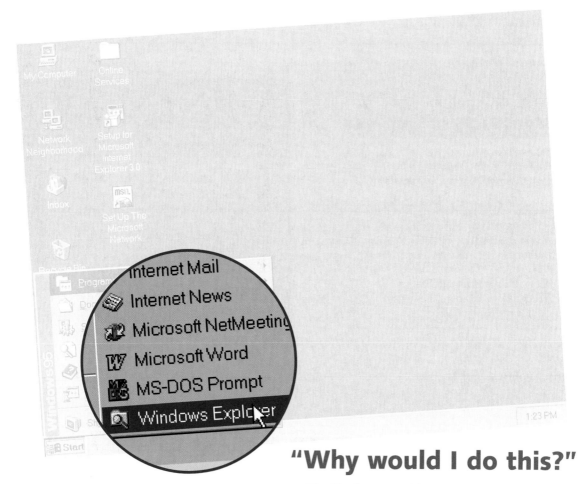

"Why would I do this?"

The Explorer enables you to open folders so you can see their contents. In addition, you can open files (such as documents or spreadsheets) from the Explorer. When you open a file in the Explorer, the application in which the file was created automatically opens, displaying the selected file, ready to edit.

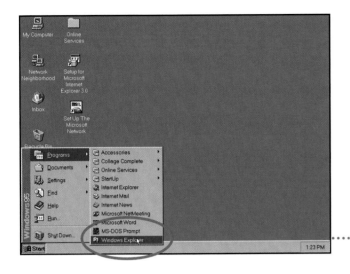

1 To open the Explorer, open the **Start** menu and choose **Programs**. From the secondary menu, choose **Windows Explorer**.

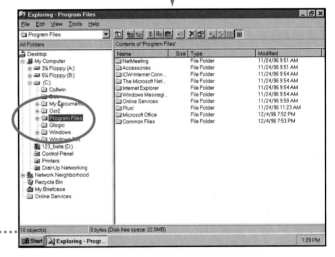

2 In the left side of the Explorer window, select the folder containing the saved file you want to open. A list of subfolders, or subdirectories, appears on the right side of the window. (Depending on the folder you select on the left side of the window, the right side may also list files stored in the folder.)

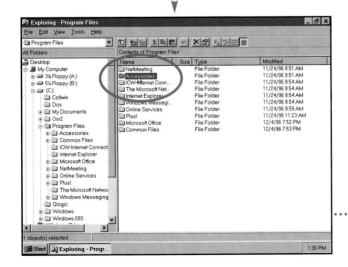

3 On the right side of the window, double-click the subfolder that contains the saved file.

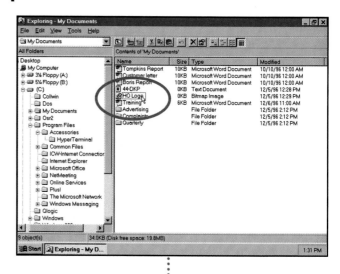

4 Double-click the file to open it within the application.

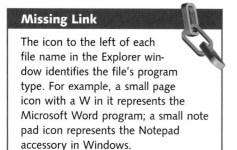

Missing Link

The icon to the left of each file name in the Explorer window identifies the file's program type. For example, a small page icon with a W in it represents the Microsoft Word program; a small note pad icon represents the Notepad accessory in Windows.

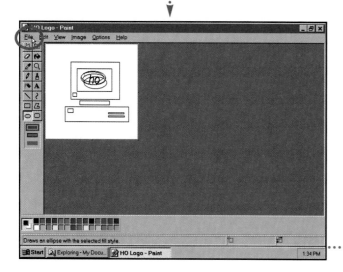

5 When you're done with the file, close the application by choosing **File**, **Exit**. If prompted by the application, choose to save the file. Windows closes the application and returns to the Windows Explorer. (As with any window, you can also close an application window by clicking the **Close** (X) button.)

6 To close the Windows Explorer, choose **File**, **Close**. ■

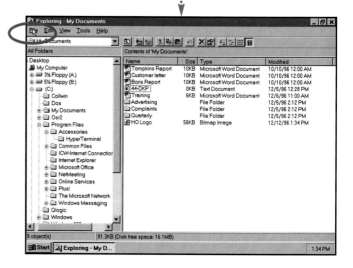

Saving Your Work

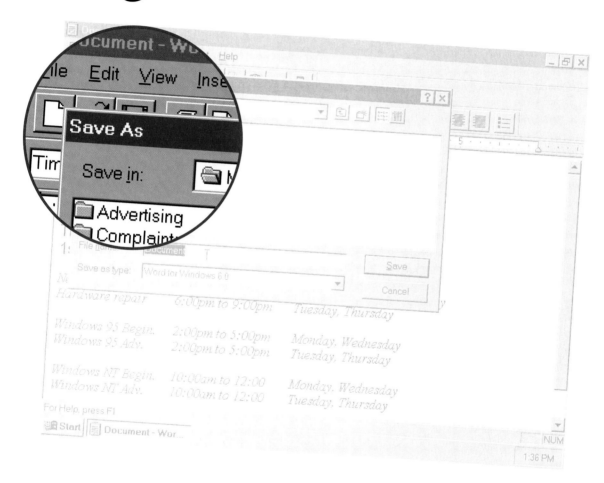

"Why would I do this?"

You save documents and files so you can refer to them later for printing, modification, copying, and so on. You save documents in much the same way in all Windows applications. This task shows you how to save a document in WordPad.

Task 22: Saving Your Work

1 Choose **Start**, **Programs**, **Accessories** and click the **WordPad** command to open WordPad. In the application, choose **File**, **Save As**. The Save As dialog box appears.

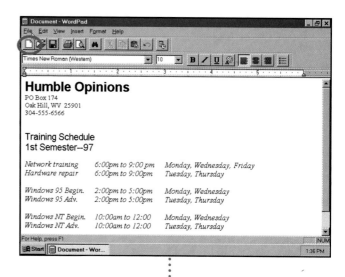

Puzzled?

Two commands on the File menu relate to saving a document. Use Save As when you want to designate a storage location or when you want to save a second copy of the file under a new name. Use the Save command when you want to save recently made changes to a file that's already been named.

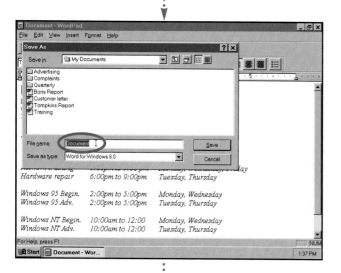

2 In the **File Name** text box, enter a name for the file you want to save. You can use spaces and other punctuation, along with numbers and letters. If you save the file in the current folder, you will always be able to find it when you need to open it later for revisions or printing.

Puzzled?

: " ? * < > / \ | .

You cannot use these characters in a file name, but you can use spaces, letters, and numbers.

3 If you want to save the file in the current folder, click the **Save** button. Alternatively, you can save the file in the My Documents folder (or some other particular folder) so all of your files will be together and easy to find. To save the file in the My Documents folder, click the **Up One Level** button. The folders on the hard drive appear in the list.

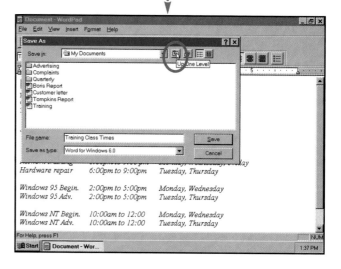

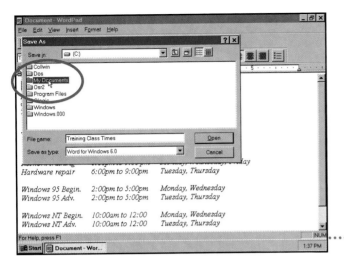

4 Double-click the **My Documents** folder.

5 The folder opens, displaying other files (if you have saved files there before). Make sure the name of your file is what you want, and then click the **Save** command button. The application saves the file and returns to the document window. ■

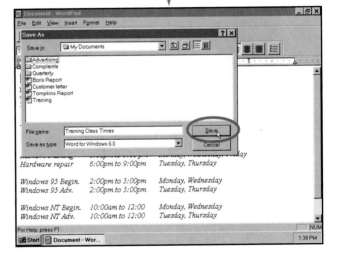

Closing an Application

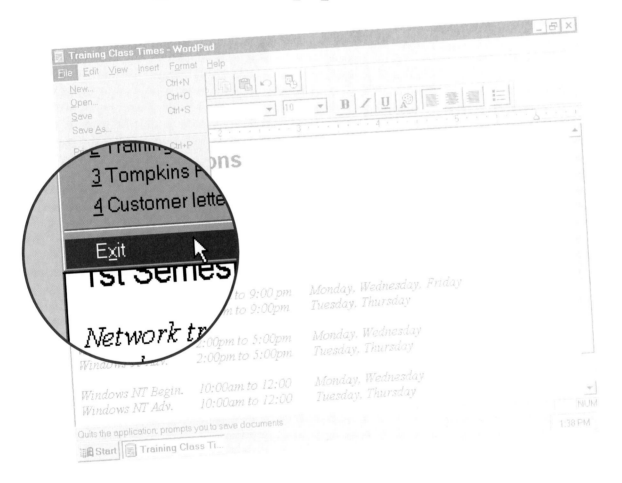

"Why would I do this?"

You can leave applications open for later use (minimize them), just as you can leave windows open. However, when you finish working in a program, you will want to close that program to free system memory. Too many open applications can tax your system's memory and slow the computer's processes, such as saving, printing, switching between applications, and so on.

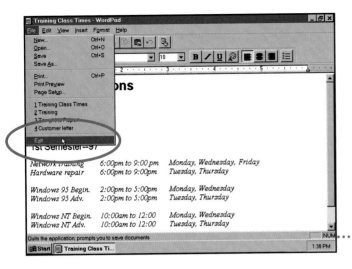

1 To close an application, open the application's **File** menu and choose the **Exit** command. Every Windows application works the same.

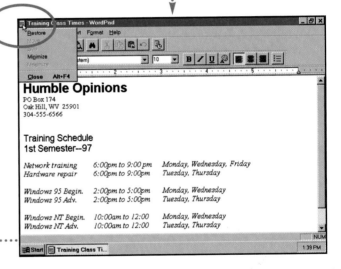

2 A second method of closing an application is to open the application's **Control** menu by clicking the icon at the far left end of the title bar. From the Control menu, choose **Close**. (Alternatively, simply press **Alt+F4**.)

3 The final method of closing an application is to click the **Close** (X) button in the application's title bar. ■

Puzzled?

If you have not saved a file and choose to close the application, a message box appears asking if you want to save. If you do, click **Yes**; if not, click **No**. If you want to return to the document, click **Cancel**.

Accessing Application Folders

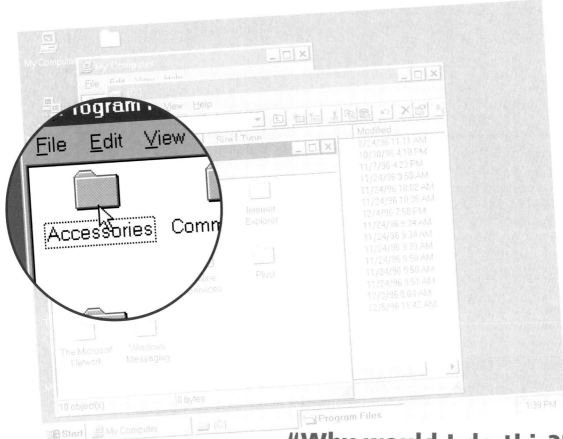

"Why would I do this?"

You can access an application's folder so you can view its contents, copy or delete its contents, or create new folders within it to hold such things as documents. A folder represents a directory; all files—whether program files, document files, or other files—are stored in a folder. Part 4 explains how to work with folders and files.

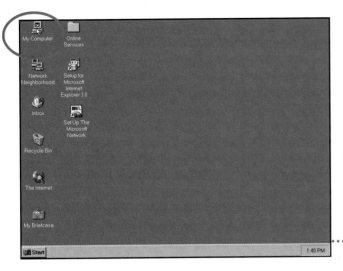

1 Open the My Computer window by double-clicking the **My Computer** icon. The My Computer window contains at least two folders (or directories): the Control Panel and the Printers folder. It may also contain the DialUp folder, which is used for remote access to a network.

2 Open the hard drive window by double-clicking the icon representing your hard drive (usually **C:**). The hard drive window lists all folders and a few files. Each folder represents directories holding related files.

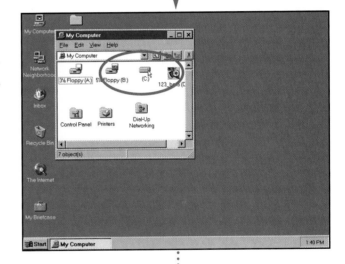

Puzzled?

If you have Microsoft or Lotus products installed on your computer, you'll likely see folders representing these applications, too (such as the Lotus Applications folder and the Microsoft Office folder). You can open these folders just as you can the Windows and Accessories folders.

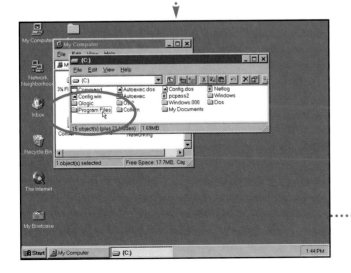

3 Open the window for the Program folder by double-clicking the **Program Files** folder icon. The Program Files folder contains the Accessories, Internet Explorer, and Online Services folders, as well as others you see when you open the Programs menu from the Start menu.

4 Double-click the **Accessories** folder, or any folder, to view its contents.

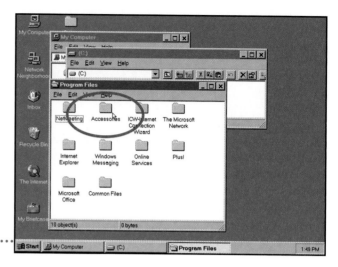

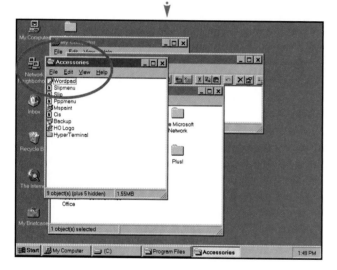

5 To view an application folder's contents, double-click its icon in the Programs window. You can use the menus of the application's window to create new folders, copy and paste an application icon elsewhere, and so on. When you finish in the application's window, click the **Close** (X) button in the title bar to close the window. If you prefer the windows closed, continue clicking the **Close** button in each window you encounter until you close all windows. ■

Adding and Using Shortcuts

"Why would I do this?"

You can create shortcuts and place them on the desktop to provide quick access for opening programs, folders, and documents. You then click a shortcut to quickly go to an item you use often—without having to open menus and folders.

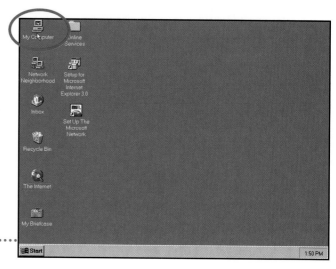

1 Open the My Computer window by double-clicking the **My Computer** icon.

2 Select the **A:** drive by clicking its icon. The icon changes color to indicate it is selected.

Puzzled?

If you do not have an A drive or a floppy disk to use in this exercise, choose the **Control Panel** folder instead of the drive icon. The rest of the exercise works exactly the same.

3 Open the **File** menu, and the menu displays a list of commands. Choose the **Create Shortcut** command.

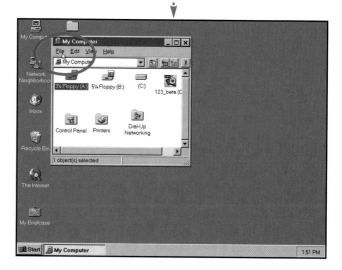

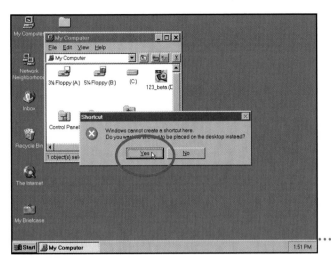

4 Insert any disk into the floppy drive. A shortcut message appears asking if you want the shortcut placed on the desktop. Choose **Yes**, and the shortcut appears on the desktop. It looks just like the item's icon with an arrow pointing to it.

5 Close the My Computer window by clicking the **Close** (X) button in the title bar.

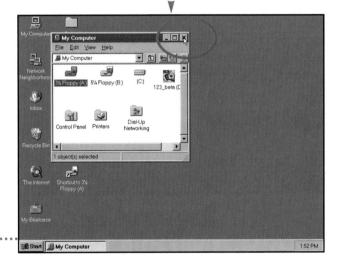

6 To quickly access drive A:, make sure you have inserted a disk in the drive, and then double-click the shortcut icon on the desktop. The floppy drive window opens, displaying the items stored on the floppy disk. ■

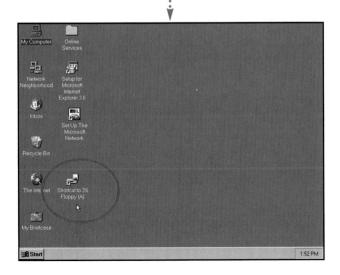

Puzzled?

You close the floppy drive window as you would any other: double-click the **Control-menu** box, or press **Alt+F4**, or click the **Close** (X) button in the title bar.

Deleting Shortcuts

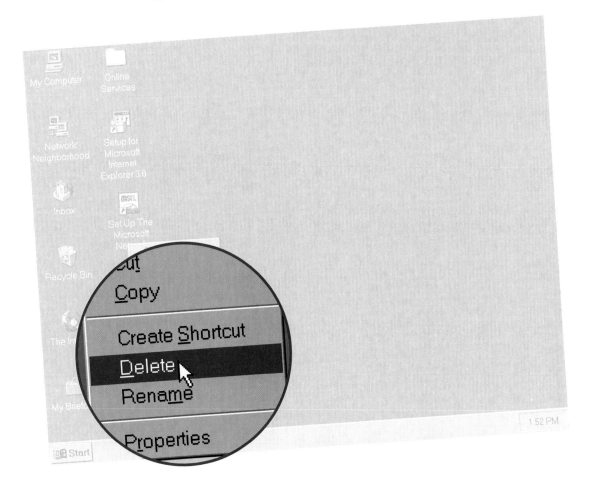

"Why would I do this?"

You use shortcuts to quickly get to the drive, document, application, or folder you use most often. As time passes, however, many of those items will change, and the desktop may become cluttered. You can always create new shortcuts as new documents or folders appear, and you can delete those shortcuts you no longer use.

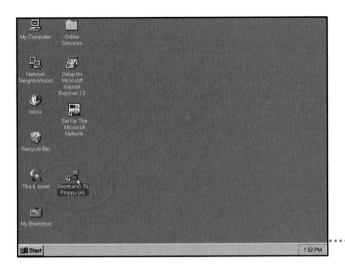

1 Select the shortcut by clicking it. The shortcut changes color.

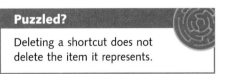

Puzzled?

Deleting a shortcut does not delete the item it represents.

2 Right-click the selected icon, and a shortcut menu appears. Choose the **Delete** command.

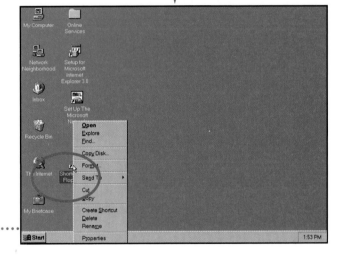

3 Windows displays a confirmation message. Click **Yes** to delete the shortcut. Windows removes the shortcut to the Recycle Bin. To truly delete the shortcut from the hard drive, you must empty the bin.

4 On the desktop, click the **Recycle Bin** to select it. The Bin icon changes color.

Missing Link

If you change your mind about deleting an item completely, you can retrieve it from the Recycle Bin. To do so, right-click the **Recycle Bin** to display the shortcut menu and choose **Open**. In the Recycle Bin window, click the item you want to restore and choose **File**, **Restore**. The item returns to its original location.

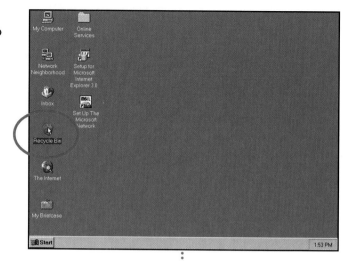

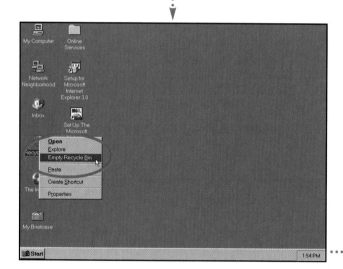

5 Right-click to display the Recycle Bin's shortcut menu. Choose **Empty Recycle Bin**. (Notice that you also could choose Open to open the Bin and view the contents, in case you've forgotten what you placed in it.)

6 Click **Yes** to delete the contents of the Bin. If you click No, the contents remain in the Bin. ■

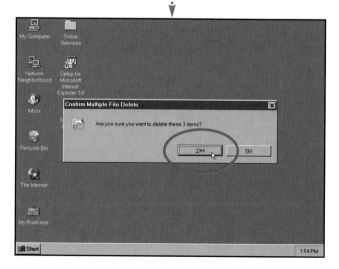

PART IV

Working with Folders and Files

A PART OF WORKING WITH WINDOWS is learning how to use the folders: a file folder icon represents a directory or subdirectory. Think of your computer's hard drive as a filing cabinet. Directories on the hard drive represent drawers in the filing cabinet, and each directory can hold subdirectories just as each filing cabinet drawer can hold manila file folders. Each manila file folder can contain other file folders or files.

Windows uses folder icons to represent directories and subdirectories. A folder can hold other folders as well as files. You can open and close folders, view a folder's contents, copy and move folders, and create or delete folders.

The more you work on your computer, the more files and folders you add. You install more program files in addition to saving document files, spreadsheet data, and the like. After a while, your computer may become cluttered, and finding a specific file may become impossible.

Windows provides features that can help you find, organize, and manage your files. Windows includes a Find feature that enables you to search anywhere in the system for one or more files. You specify where you want to search (hard drive, floppy drive, CD, and so on), and then you enter search criteria (usually the file name). When you give Windows the go-ahead to find the file, it searches the specified area for your file.

After you find files, you can copy and paste them to other drives or folders. Cutting and pasting a file moves it to another area on the disk. When you copy or cut a file or folder, Windows places it on the Clipboard, a temporary storage area. Then you can choose to paste the file or folder to a new location. A copy of the item remains on the Clipboard until you copy or cut another item. You can paste an item over and over again from the Clipboard.

Windows also stores your programs and document files in folders that you can view in My Computer and in the Windows Explorer. In previous versions of Windows, folders were called directories. You can create folders within folders in Windows 95 just as you could create subdirectories within directories in earlier versions. Additionally, you can store files in folders, and you can copy and move files from folder to folder.

My Computer is a window containing icons that represent your hard drive, floppy drives, tape and CD drives, and so on. You can open the hard drive, for example, to view the contents, modify the folders, add new folders, and otherwise manipulate and modify the folders in your computer. You learned to open My Computer and your hard drive window in Part 1.

The Explorer is the Windows 95 version of the File Manager from Windows 3.x, and it works similarly. You access the Explorer by opening the **Start** menu and choosing **Programs**, **Windows Explorer**. In the Explorer, you can view and select folders, add new folders, rename folders and files, and otherwise manipulate the contents just like in the My Computer window. One major difference between My Computer and the Explorer is that in the Explorer you can view all folders in one part of the window while viewing a specific folder's contents in another part of the window—which makes copying and moving files easier.

TASK

Opening Folders

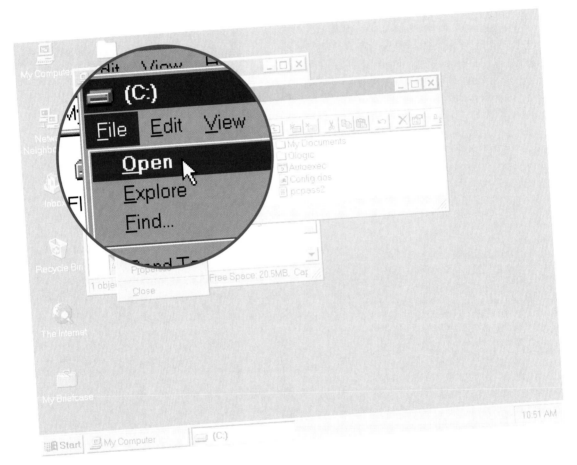

"Why would I do this?"

Folders contain files, programs, or other items you can use to do work in Windows. When you open a folder, you reveal the folder's contents in a window.

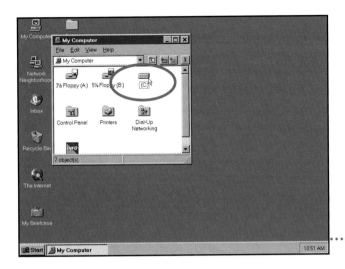

1 Double-click the **My Computer** icon on the desktop. The My Computer window opens. In the My Computer window, double-click the icon representing your hard drive (usually **C:**). The drive window appears, with icons representing folders (directories) on your hard drive.

2 Select the **Dos** folder in the drive window by clicking the folder icon once. That icon appears in a different color.

Missing Link

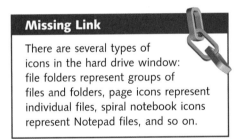

There are several types of icons in the hard drive window: file folders represent groups of files and folders, page icons represent individual files, spiral notebook icons represent Notepad files, and so on.

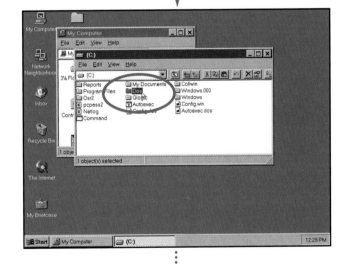

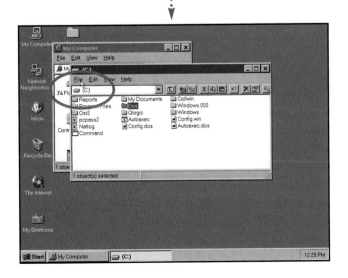

3 Open the **File** menu and choose the **Open** command. The Dos folder opens in a separate window. (As an alternative to steps 2 and 3, you can double-click the folder to open it.) ■

TASK 28

Creating a Folder

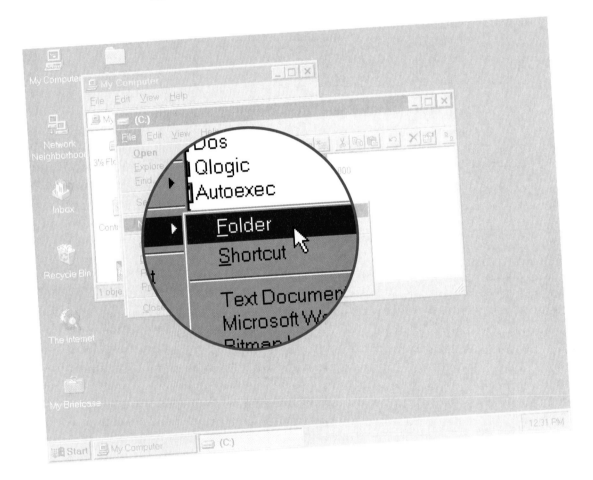

"Why would I do this?"

Working with your files is easier if you group related files into folders. For example, you may want to create a folder in your word processing program's folder to hold all the documents you create with that program. Creating a folder enables you to keep your documents separated from the program's files so you can easily find what you need to do your work.

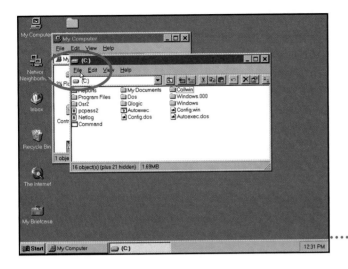

1 Open the window for the folder or disk where you want to create the new folder. For example, open the window for your hard drive. Then open the **File** menu and choose the **New** command. A secondary menu appears.

2 From the secondary menu, choose the **Folder** command. The new folder appears in the drive window.

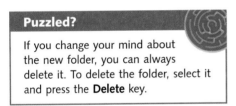

> **Puzzled?**
>
> If you change your mind about the new folder, you can always delete it. To delete the folder, select it and press the **Delete** key.

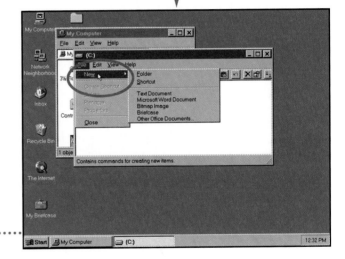

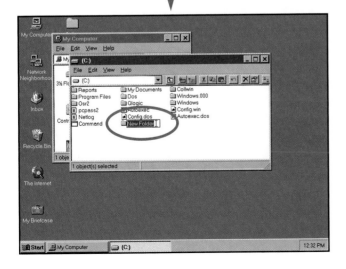

3 The folder's name is highlighted: **New Folder**. When you type, the mouse pointer changes to an I-beam, and the name of the folder becomes highlighted. Enter a new name for the folder. When you finish typing, press **Enter** to accept the new name. ■

Copying Folders

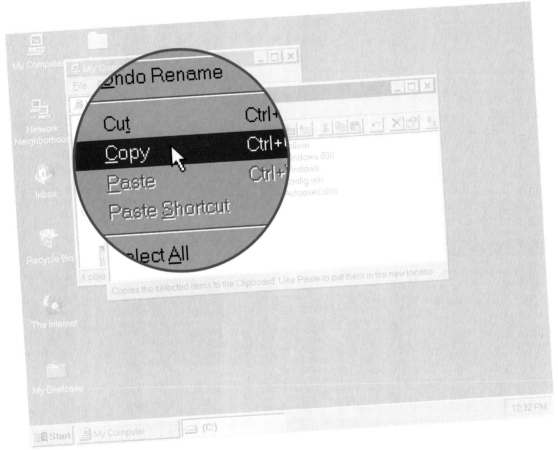

"Why would I do this?"

Windows makes it easy for you to copy a folder and its contents and then paste them in a new location. You can, for example, copy a folder to a floppy disk to use as a backup or to move to another computer. In addition, you can copy a folder and its contents to another location on the hard drive if, for example, you want to revise the original file for a different use.

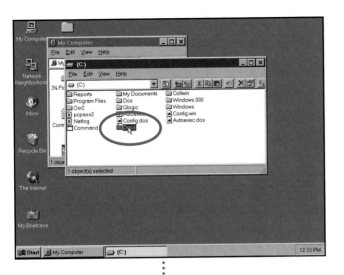

1 Insert a floppy disk in your A or B drive. In your hard drive window, select the folder you want to copy. For this example, select the new folder you created in the last task.

Missing Link

To copy more than one folder at a time, hold the **Ctrl** key and then click each folder you want to copy. Release the Ctrl key before you choose the Copy command.

2 Open the **Edit** menu and choose the **Copy** command to copy the folder to the Windows storage area called the *Clipboard*. The menu closes.

Missing Link

You can also copy a folder by first opening both the window that contains the folder (the source) and the window to which you want to copy the folder (the destination). Then click the folder in the source window and drag it to the destination window.

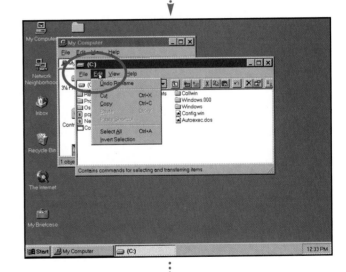

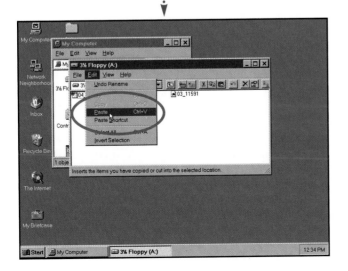

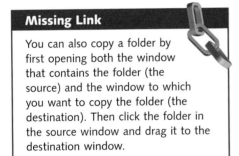

3 In the My Computer window, double-click the drive icon for your floppy disk (or an alternate location on your hard drive) to open it. In the floppy drive window, open the **Edit** menu and choose **Paste**. Windows copies the new folder and its contents from the Clipboard to the floppy disk. As Windows copies the folder, a message box appears; when the box disappears, the copy and paste procedure is complete. ■

Moving Folders

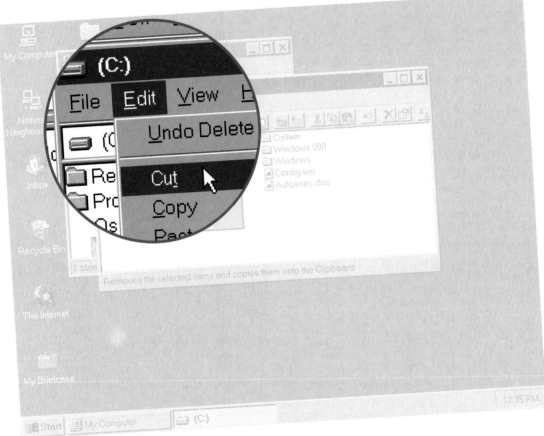

"Why would I do this?"

You can move a folder and its contents to another folder or to a disk so you can reorganize your directory structure. Suppose, for example, you want to move all related files and folders to the same place on your hard drive so you can find them quickly and easily. You can move all of those folders to one folder for better organization of your hard drive.

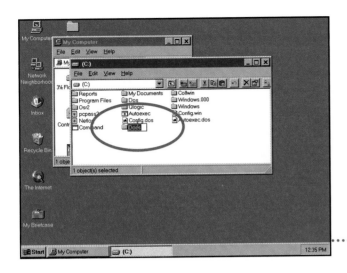

1 Select the new folder you created earlier (the Docs folder in this example).

2 Open the **Edit** menu and choose the **Cut** command to move the folder. The menu closes, and only a ghost of the cut folder shows in the window. The folder is moved to the Windows Clipboard until you're ready to paste it.

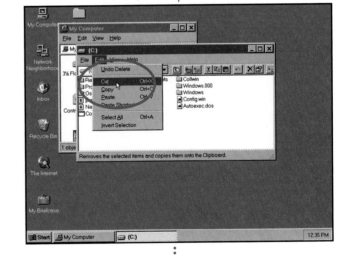

Missing Link

To move more than one file or folder at a time, hold the **Ctrl** key and then click each file or folder. Release the Ctrl key before you choose the Cut command.

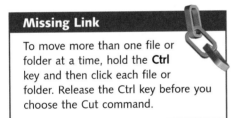

3 Double-click the **My Documents** folder in your hard drive window. In the My Documents window, open the **Edit** menu and choose **Paste**. Windows moves the folder from the Clipboard to the My Documents folder. ■

Missing Link

You can move a folder by opening the window containing the folder (the source) and the window to which you will move the folder (the destination). Then press and hold the **Shift** key and drag the folder to the destination window.

83

TASK 31

Renaming Folders

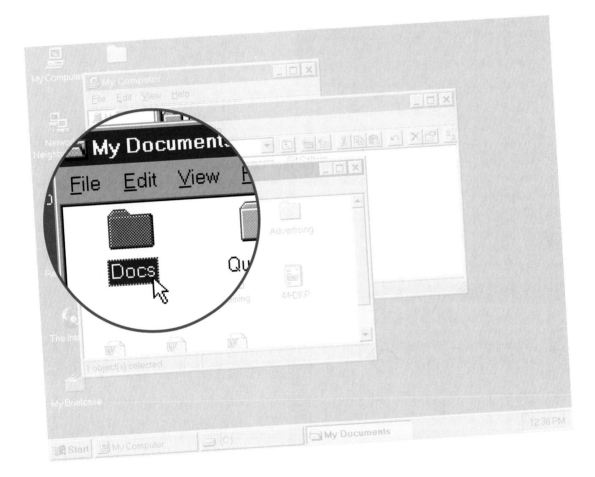

"Why would I do this?"

As you add more and more folders and files to
your computer, you will eventually need to
rearrange and reorganize folders and files.
Windows lets you easily rename folders to help
you better organize your computer work.

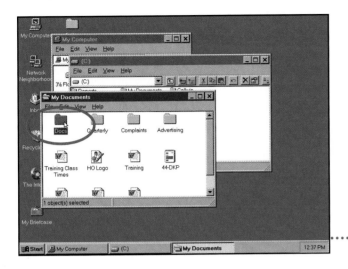

1 Click the folder once to select it, and the folder changes color.

2 Click the folder's name to display the mouse I-beam and to select the folder's name.

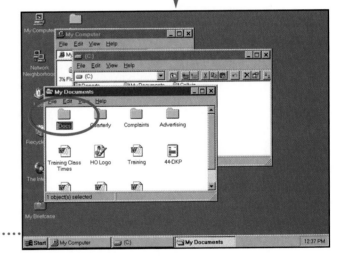

3 Enter a new name for the folder and press **Enter** to accept the name. ■

Missing Link

When naming or renaming folders or files, you can use a name containing up to 255 characters, including spaces. You also can include letters, numbers, and other symbols on your keyboard, with the exception of the following:

| ? / : " * < > \ | .

85

Deleting Folders

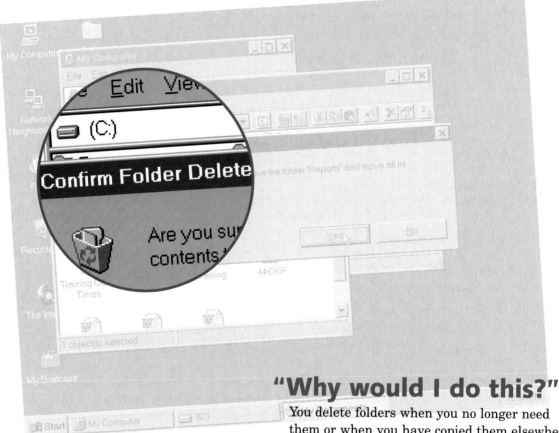

"Why would I do this?"

You delete folders when you no longer need them or when you have copied them elsewhere as a backup and do not need two copies. When you delete a folder from your hard drive, remember that you also delete its contents. Windows removes deleted folders to the Recycle Bin. You can change your mind and restore deleted items from the Recycle Bin if you make a mistake. (See Task 26 in Part 3 for information about emptying the Recycle Bin and restoring items in the Recycle Bin.) Take note that when you delete a folder from a floppy drive, that item is deleted immediately, without going first to the Recycle Bin.

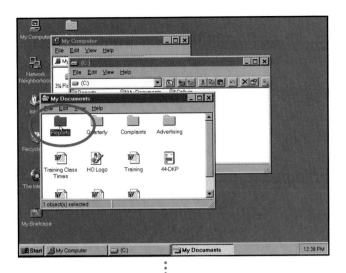

1 Select the folder you want to delete. The selected folder changes color.

Missing Link

To select multiple folders, hold the **Ctrl** key and click each folder you want to select. To deselect one folder of several, hold the **Ctrl** key and click the folder you want to deselect. To deselect all folders, click anywhere in the window.

2 Open the **File** menu and choose the **Delete** command. A confirmation message appears.

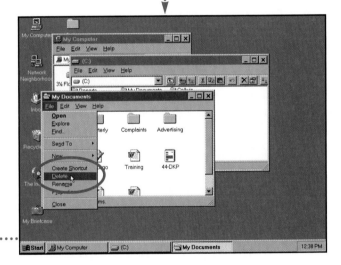

3 Click **Yes** to delete the selected folder; the confirmation box closes, and the folder disappears. ■

Puzzled?

If you change your mind about deleting the folder, click the **No** button in the Confirm Folder Delete message box. The box closes, and you're returned to the intact folder.

TASK

33

Finding Files and Folders

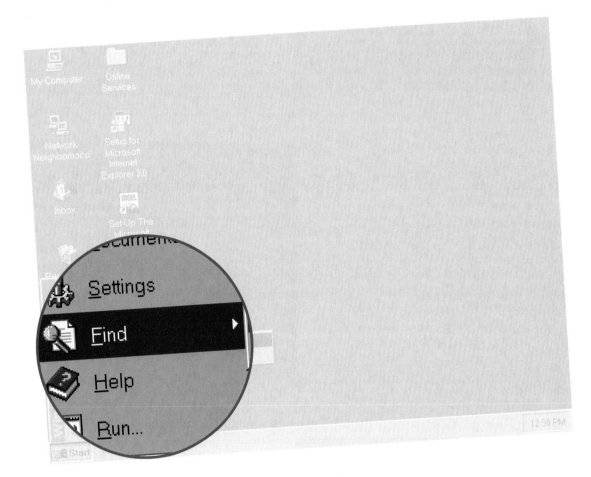

"Why would I do this?"

After working for months with your applications, your computer becomes filled with various folders and files, which can make it nearly impossible for you to know where everything is. Luckily, Windows includes a command that helps you locate specific files or folders by name, file type, location of the file, and so on.

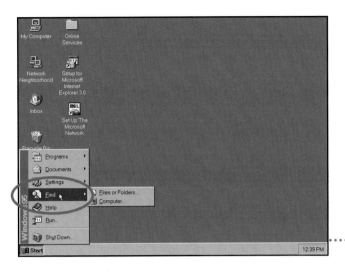

1 Open the **Start** menu and choose the **Find** command. A secondary menu appears. From the secondary menu, choose **Files or Folders**. The Find: All Files dialog box appears.

2 Click the **Name & Location** tab. Then, in the **Named** text box, enter the name of the file you want to search for.

Missing Link

You can use the characters *
and ? (known as *wild cards*) in
the search. For example, to find all
files ending with the extension .HLP,
you could type ***.hlp**. Similarly, you
could type **doc??.*** to find all files
beginning with doc, followed by any
two characters and ending in any
extension.

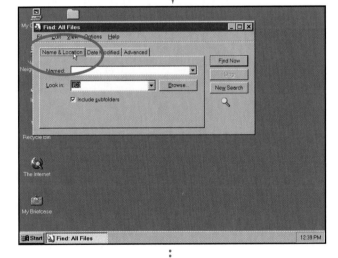

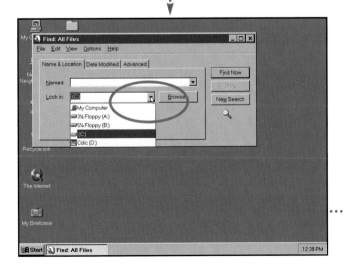

3 To change the drive on which Windows will conduct the search, click the down arrow next to the **Look In** list box and choose the floppy or CD-ROM drive from the drop-down list. If you want to narrow the search area even more, you can choose **Browse** and then double-click a specific folder in the Browse for Folder dialog box.

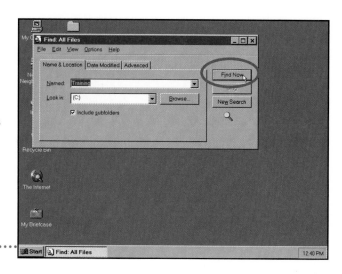

4 Click the **Find Now** button to initiate the search for the file name. Windows searches the hard drive by default and displays a list of found files at the bottom of the dialog box.

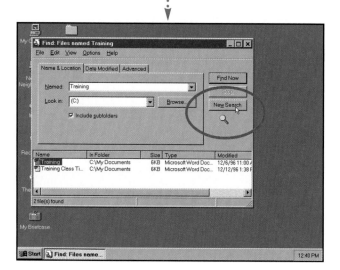

5 Click the **New Search** button to search for another file or folder. A warning message appears, stating that the previous search will be cleared. Click **OK**, and the Find box appears, ready for the next search. To close the Find dialog box, click the **Close** (X) button in the title bar. ■

Puzzled?

If you do not know the name of the file for which you are searching but you know what type of file it is, click the **Advanced** tab in the Find dialog box. From the **Of Type** list box, choose the type of file you're searching for (such as Application, Configuration, Help, Microsoft Word Document, or Text Document). Click the **Find Now** button, and Windows performs the search.

Managing Folders with the Shortcut Menu

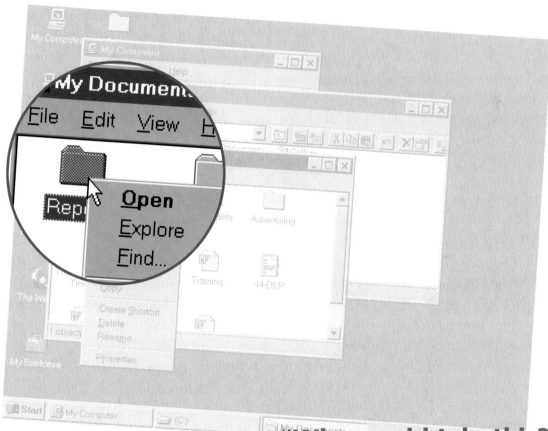

"Why would I do this?"

Use the shortcut menu to cut, copy, or paste a folder to another location, to rename or delete a folder, or to create a shortcut for the folder. Managing folders using the shortcut menu makes your work faster and easier.

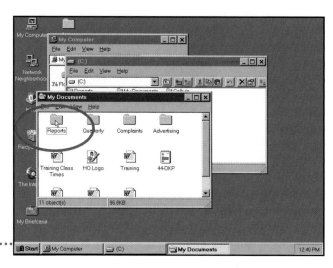

1 To display a folder's shortcut menu, right-click the folder. The quick menu appears.

2 Choose **Send To**, and a secondary menu appears. Select the floppy drive to which you want to send a copy of the folder, and Windows copies the folder. From the same shortcut menu, you can also use the following commands to manage your folders: **Delete** deletes the folder and its contents; **Create Shortcut** creates a shortcut icon you can drag to the desktop for quick and easy folder access; **Cut** and **Copy** move or copy the selected folder to the Windows Clipboard. (Open another folder or drive on your computer and choose the **Paste** command from the shortcut menu to paste a folder to that new location.)

3 Right-click a folder to display the shortcut menu, and then choose the **Rename** command. Windows selects the folder's name; all you have to do is type in the new name. ■

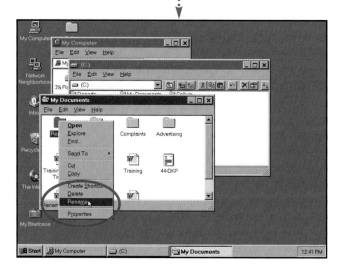

Using the Toolbar

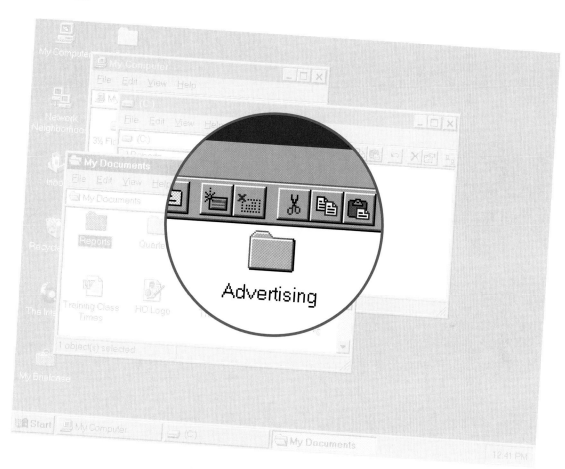

"Why would I do this?"

Each window, whether it's a file or folder window, includes a toolbar you can use to quickly change drives or directories in the window and to change views of the folder contents. (Note that the Windows Explorer displays this toolbar by default.)

1 Open a window for your computer's hard drive, and then open the **My Documents** window. Folders icons represent the directories in the My Documents folder.

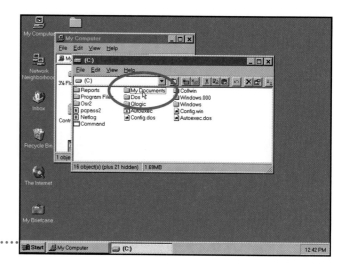

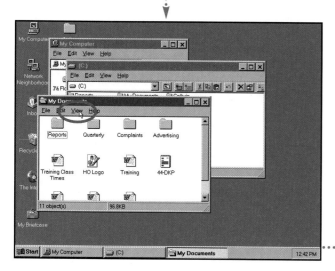

2 Choose the **View**, **Toolbar** command, and Windows adds a toolbar to the window (below the menu bar). To view the entire toolbar, you may need to resize the window.

3 Click the down arrow next to the **Go to a Different Folder** list box to view the available drives. You can change drives, or you can work within the current drive. ■

Puzzled?

If you are not sure what a button on the toolbar does, hold the mouse pointer over the button. A ToolTip appears, describing the function of the button.

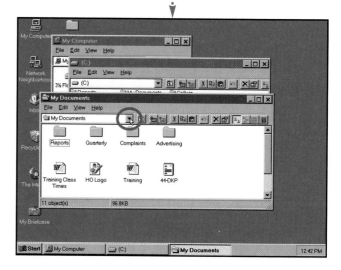

Sorting Files

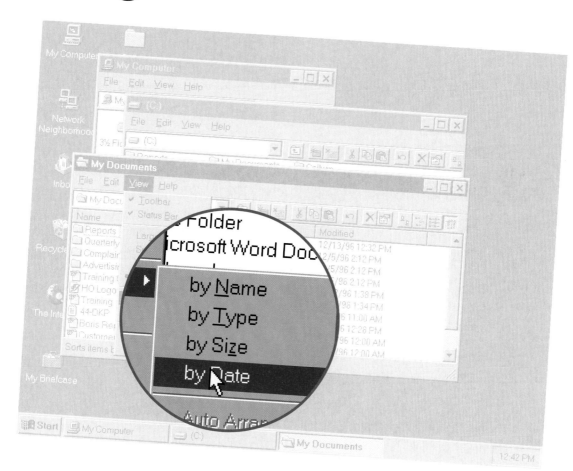

"Why would I do this?"

You sort the files in a folder so you can more easily find the files you want. Windows enables you to arrange the files in a folder by name, type, date, and size. Sorting the files is even easier if you choose to view them by the file details first. You can sort files viewed as large or small icons or as a list.

1 Open the folder or drive containing the files you want to sort. Choose **View**, **Details** to list the file names, sizes, and types. Enlarge the window, if necessary, to see all of the file details.

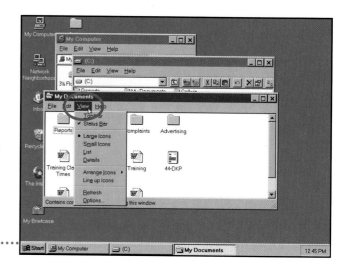

2 Choose **View**, **Arrange Icons**, and a secondary menu appears. Choose **By Size** to sort the files from the smallest to largest.

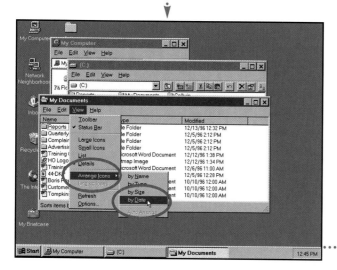

3 Alternatively, you can click the **Size** button above the list of files to sort by size; click the **Size** button again, and Windows re-sorts the files from largest to smallest. ■

Missing Link

You can also sort by name in alphabetical order, by file type, or by date from oldest to most recent by choosing the appropriate command from the View, Arrange Icons submenu.

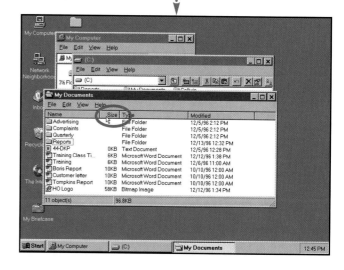

Copying and Moving Files

"Why would I do this?"

Windows makes it easy to copy and move files from one folder to another and from one disk to another. You have the choice of using the Edit menu, a shortcut menu, or keyboard shortcuts; you can also simply drag the files to their new locations. You might copy files in order to create a backup copy or to revise one copy while keeping the original file intact. You might move files to reorganize folders or to make more room on your hard drive.

1 First, select the file you want to copy. Then choose **Edit**, **Copy** to duplicate the file or **Edit**, **Cut** to move the file.

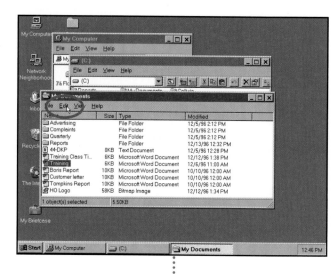

Missing Link

To use drag-and-drop editing to move and copy files, open the window that contains the file and the window for the folder or drive you want to put it in. To move the file, hold the **Shift** key and drag the file to its destination. To copy a file, hold the **Ctrl** key and drag the file to its destination.

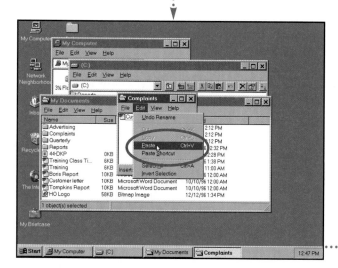

2 Select the folder, drive, or window into which you want to paste the copied or moved file and choose **Edit**, **Paste**. Windows copies or moves the file to the new location.

Puzzled?

By default, if you drag a file to a folder on the same disk, it will be moved; if you drag a file to a folder on a different disk, it will be copied.

3 To copy a file to a floppy disk, right-click the selected file. The shortcut menu appears. Choose **Send To** and then choose the appropriate floppy drive. ■

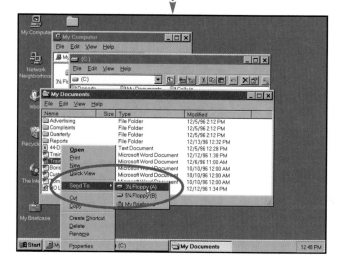

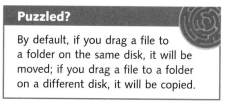

Deleting a File

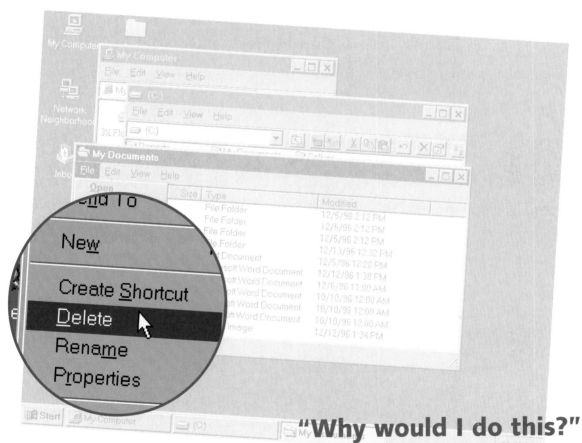

"Why would I do this?"

Eventually, your computer will become full of files, and you'll have a hard time organizing and storing them all. You can copy necessary files to floppy disks, tapes, and so on, and then delete the files from your hard drive to make room for new files. In addition, you will sometimes want to delete files you no longer need.

1 Select the file you want to delete, and then choose **File**, **Delete**.

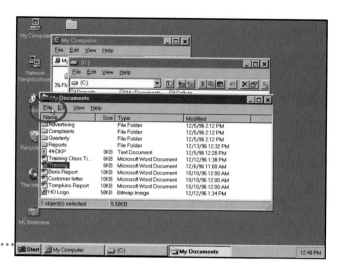

2 Windows displays the Confirm File Delete dialog box. Click **Yes** to delete the file. Windows removes the file from its current location and places it in the Recycle Bin.

Missing Link

If you change your mind about deleting objects in the Recycle Bin, right-click the **Bin** icon and choose **Open** from the shortcut menu. A list of objects in the Bin appears. Select the item you want to keep and choose **File**, **Restore**. The file is returned to its original location.

3 To empty the Recycle Bin, right-click the **Recycle Bin** icon. From the shortcut menu that appears, choose **Empty Recycle Bin**. Windows displays the Confirm File Delete dialog box again; click **Yes** to delete the file. ■

Puzzled?

After you empty the Recycle Bin, you cannot restore the files that were in it.

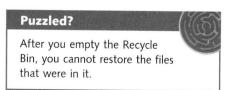

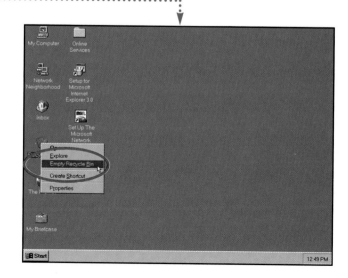

Using the Windows Explorer

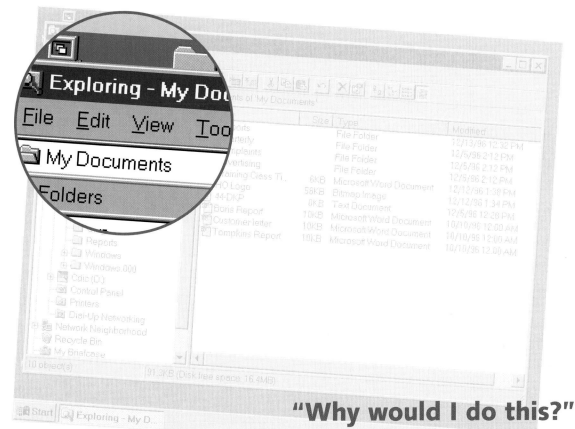

"Why would I do this?"

You can use the Windows Explorer in much the same way you use the My Computer window: to copy and move folders, create and rename folders, view details, and so on. You might be more comfortable using the Explorer if you have used Windows 3.0 or 3.1 because the Explorer in Windows 95 is very similar to the File Manager in previous versions of Windows. Alternatively, you might simply prefer the appearance of the Windows Explorer to that of the My Computer window.

1 To open the Windows Explorer, open the **Start** menu and choose **Programs** from the menu. From the Programs menu, choose **Windows Explorer**.

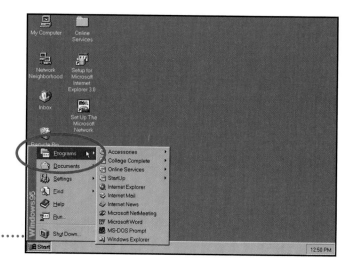

2 The left side of the split Explorer window lists all drives and folders on the hard drive. Any folder with a plus sign (+) in front of it contains more folders and files. Click the folder, and the folder's contents appear on the right side of the Explorer window. Double-click the folder, and any folders it contains also appear under it on the left side of the window.

3 Double-click any folder on the right side of the Explorer window to display the contents of that folder. If you double-click a file (such as a document file or a program file), Windows opens that file and/or application. When you display a folder's contents on the right side of the Explorer window, file details appear by default.

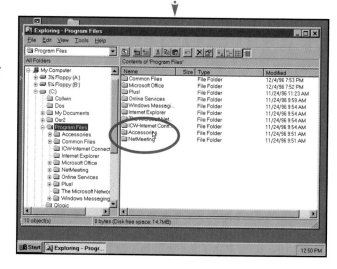

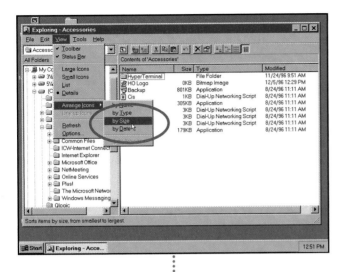

4 To sort the files by type, date, size, or name, choose **View**, **Arrange Icons**, and select the appropriate sort type.

> **Missing Link**
>
> The View menu also provides commands with which you can show the files as large or small icons, display or hide the toolbar, and display or hide the status bar of the Explorer window. Additionally, you can use the commands on the Edit menu to cut, copy, and paste any folder or file.

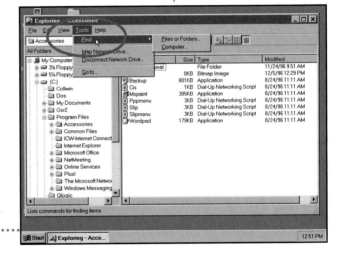

5 To search for a file in Windows Explorer, choose **Tools**, **Find** and select **Files or Folders**. The Find: All Files dialog box appears. From here, you search for any file or folder using the same procedure you learned in Task 33.

6 In Windows Explorer, you can copy and move files by dragging. Drag a file from the right side of the Explorer window to the left side and drop it on top of the folder you want to copy or move it to. When you drag a file to another drive, Windows copies the file; when you drag the file to another folder, Windows moves it. As you drag the file, a ghost outline of the file moves with the mouse. When you release the mouse button, the file is dropped (or copied) to the last location of the mouse. If the Confirm File Move dialog box appears, click **OK** to complete the move. ■

PART V

Printing with Windows

WHEN YOU FIRST INSTALL WINDOWS, it configures your printer. All Windows applications use the same Windows configuration for your printer, which saves time and ensures that you can print from any Windows application without reconfiguring for each program. Naturally, you can configure one or several printers in Windows and choose the printer you want to use at any given time. In addition, you can easily manage printing for all of your applications through Windows.

You print a document from the application in which you created it. For example, if you produce a report in Excel or Word for Windows, you print the open document from within that application. You can also print a Web document from Internet Explorer, which uses an interface and print dialog box similar to other Windows products and accessories.

When you send a file to the printer, the file first goes to a *print queue*, or holding area. Windows creates a print queue for each printer connected to your computer, and you can view file names in the print queue while they're waiting to be printed.

The print queue can contain one or many files at any time, and Windows gives you control over them. While a file is in the print queue, you can pause printing, restart printing, and even cancel the printing.

In addition to letting you manage the print queue and printing, Windows enables you to easily add printers to your computer by using a step-by-step guide called a *wizard*. The wizard guides you through installing the hardware and any drivers that may come with your printer so you are sure the printer is configured correctly. And you can just as easily remove a printer as add one.

When you have two or more printers attached to your computer and configured in Windows, you can choose one to be the default printer. The default printer is the printer that you commonly use and that your applications will print to unless otherwise directed. It is a simple procedure to change which printer is the default printer.

Finally, Windows enables you to easily change printer settings, such as the port and driver, as well as paper source, paper size, and orientation. In addition, you can modify printer settings specific to your printer; for example, PostScript printers use options such as the level of PostScript used and timeout values.

Windows makes configuring one printer for all Windows applications easy and efficient. This part shows you how to control and manage printing in Windows.

TASK

40

Printing a Document

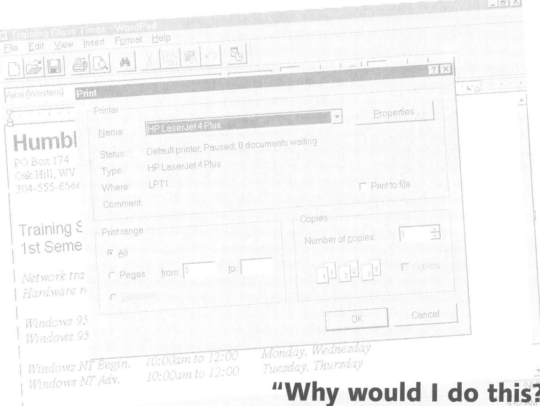

"Why would I do this?"

You can print documents from any Windows application, such as Word, Excel, Illustrator, and more, using the Windows setup for your printer. Printing your documents gives you a paper copy you can proofread, use in reports, give to coworkers, and so on.

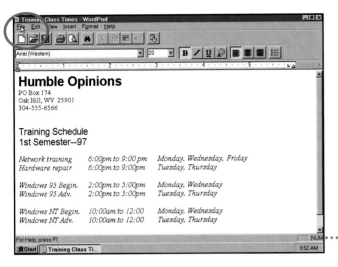

1 In the Windows application, open the **File** menu and choose the **Print** command. (The application may also provide a short-cut such as the key combination Ctrl+P.) The Print dialog box for the application opens. Each application's Print dialog box is slightly different, yet they all work basically the same.

2 Enter the number of copies, the page range, and any other specific options you want to use. Choose the printer you want to use from the **Name** drop-down list if you have more than one printer connected. Choose the **Properties** button to display a dialog box and set options specific to the selected printer.

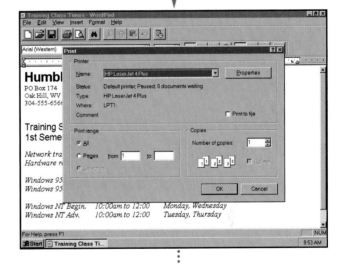

Missing Link

In most applications, you can choose **File**, **Print Preview** to preview a document before you print it.

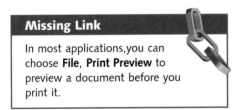

3 Click **OK** to print the document. The Print dialog box closes, and the document is sent to your printer. ■

Missing Link

You can create a shortcut for printing by opening the Printers folder from the My Computer folder. Right-click the printer icon, and a shortcut menu appears. Click **Create Shortcut**. Then drag any document icon to the printer icon for quick printing.

TASK

41

Viewing the Print Queue

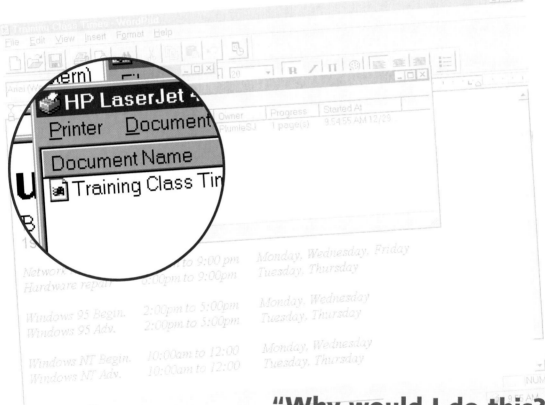

"Why would I do this?"

The print queue lists the documents that you have sent to a printer, and it shows how far along the printing is. Using the print queue, you can pause, restart, or cancel print jobs. This task shows how to view the print queue.

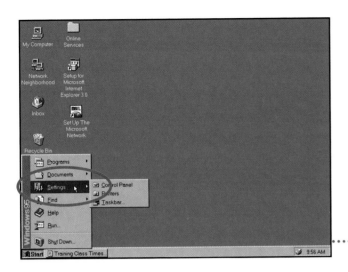

1 Open the **Start** menu and choose **Settings**. From the secondary menu that appears, choose **Printers**. The Printers window appears.

2 Double-click the printer whose print queue you want to view. The printer window opens, displaying a list of the documents in the queue plus statistics about the documents being printed. If the window is empty, there is nothing in the print queue.

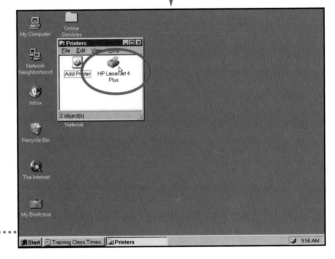

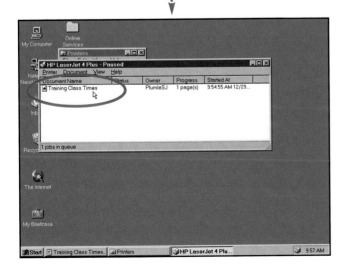

3 Using the print queue, you can pause printing one of many print jobs or all print jobs, which you'll learn in Task 43. You also can cancel printing in the print queue, as you'll learn in Task 44. To close the print queue, click the **Close** (X) button in the window's title bar. ■

Setting the Default Printer

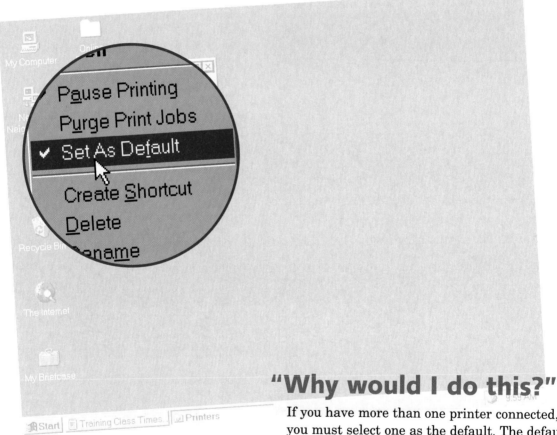

"Why would I do this?"

If you have more than one printer connected, you must select one as the default. The default printer you set in Windows is the printer your applications automatically use when you choose to print. The default printer is the one you want most of your documents printed on. This task shows you how to set the default printer in Windows.

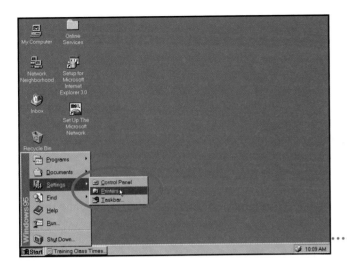

1 Open the **Start** menu and choose **Settings**. From the secondary menu, choose the **Printers** folder. The Printers window appears.

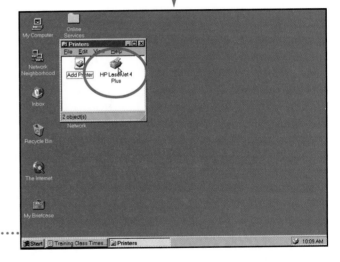

2 In the Printers window, select the printer you want to choose as the default.

3 Choose **File**, **Set As Default**. You'll see a check mark beside this command whenever you select that particular printer and pull down the File menu. ■

111

TASK 43

Pausing and Restarting the Printer

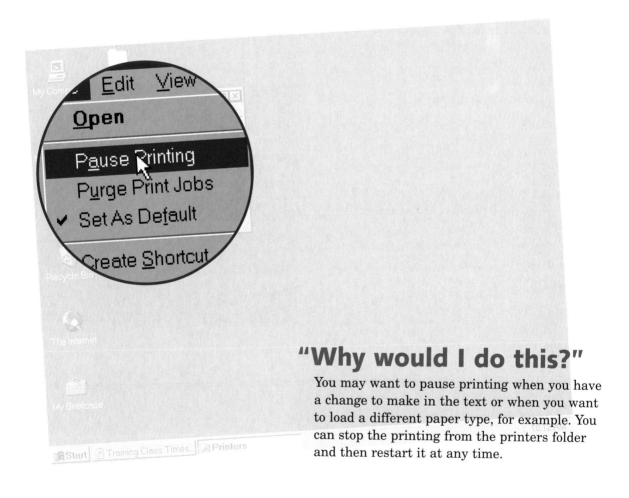

"Why would I do this?"

You may want to pause printing when you have a change to make in the text or when you want to load a different paper type, for example. You can stop the printing from the printers folder and then restart it at any time.

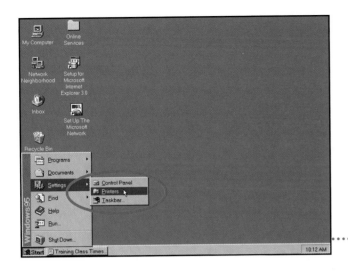

1 After sending the job to the printer, open the Printers folder by clicking the **Start** button and choosing **Settings**. Then choose **Printers** and select the printer to which you are printing.

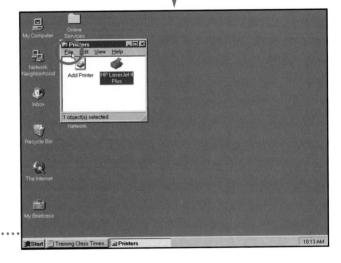

2 Open the **File** menu and choose **Pause Printing**.

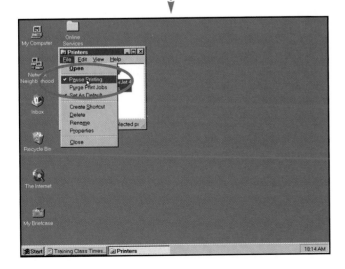

3 To restart the printing of a paused job, repeat step 1 to open the Printers folder and select the printer you want to restart. Open the **File** menu and choose **Pause Printing** to remove the check mark that's beside the command and continue printing. ■

113

Canceling Printing

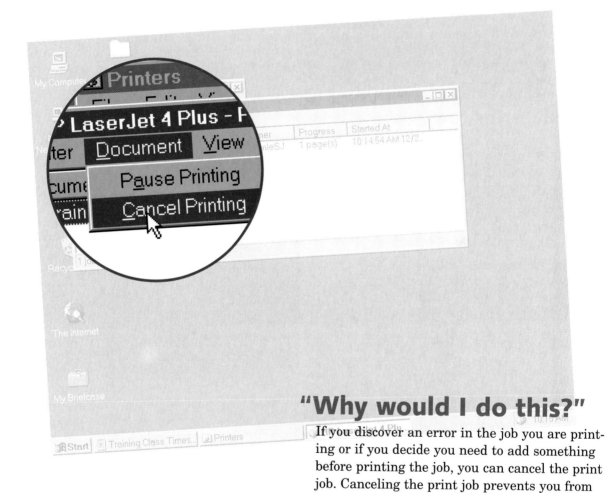

"Why would I do this?"

If you discover an error in the job you are printing or if you decide you need to add something before printing the job, you can cancel the print job. Canceling the print job prevents you from wasting time and paper.

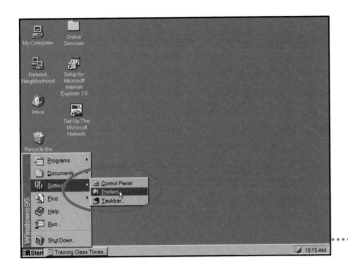

1 Open the **Start** menu and choose **Settings**. Then choose the **Printers** folder. The Printers folder window appears.

2 In the Printers folder window, double-click the printer to which the job has been sent. The print queue window for that printer opens.

Puzzled?

Depending on your computer and your printer, the print job may only be listed in the print queue for a few seconds before it is sent to the printer.

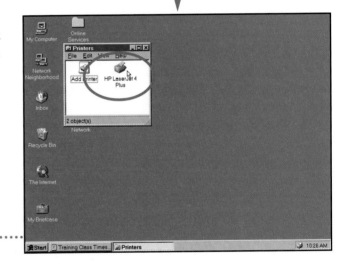

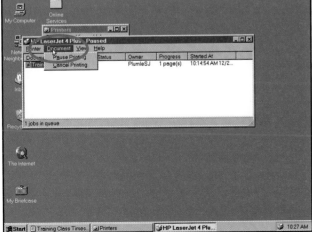

3 In the print queue, select the print job you want to cancel. Then open the **Document** menu and choose **Cancel Printing**. ■

Missing Link

You can also use the Document menu in the print queue to pause printing on a specific job (if, for example, you have sent several jobs to the printer but want to pause and change paper for a particular job). Select the job you want to pause and choose **Document**, **Pause Printing**.

Changing Printer Settings

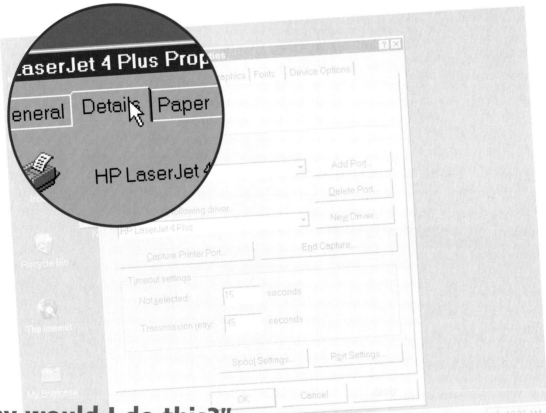

"Why would I do this?"

You can change printer settings, such as the
port, driver, and job priority as well as other
settings specific to your printer. You might, for
example, switch to a new printer driver so your
printer works better with your applications; or
you may change the port to which your printer
connects to make room for another external
device, such as a modem or tape drive. Printer
settings enable you to modify the way your
Windows printer is set up and thus the way the
printer responds to all Windows applications.

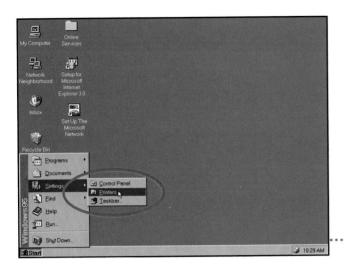

1 Open the **Start** menu, choose **Settings**, and select the **Printers** folder. The Printers folder window opens.

2 In the Printers folder window, select the printer for which you want to change settings. Then open the **File** menu and choose **Properties**. The printer's Properties dialog box that appears has various tabs that enable you to change settings.

> **Missing Link**
>
> Changing the printer's properties changes them for all documents you print on this printer. If you want to change properties for just one document, use the Page Settings or Print Setup command in the particular program.

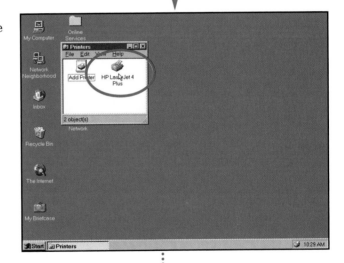

3 Choose the **Details** tab. (The number and title of tab settings on this screen will vary.) Use the upper drop-down list to select from common ports. If you choose to print to a file, Windows will prompt you for a location and file name. Choose which driver to use from the lower drop-down list, or click the **New Driver** button to install a new driver. Timeout settings specify how long Windows will wait before reporting an error to you.

4 Click the **Paper** tab to change the paper size, orientation, source, number of copies, and so on.

Puzzled?

If you make a change in the Paper, Graphics, Fonts, or Device Options tab and change your mind about the changes, you can choose the Restore Defaults button in that tab to cancel just that tab's changes.

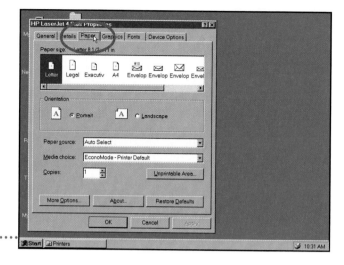

5 Choose the **Graphics** tab to change print resolution, dithering, shading intensity, and graphics mode.

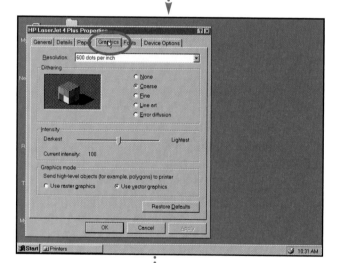

Dithering blends colors into patterns or black and white into gray for smoother printing. You can choose from various options to show sharp edges (Line Art) or smooth edges (Fine). Choose vector graphics to speed up printing but create less-detailed images; choose raster graphics to sharpen overlaid colors and details. Specify the intensity to tell Windows how dark or light to print the graphics.

6 To print a test page from the selected printer, click the **General** tab and click the **Print Test Page** button. Click **OK** when you're finished. ■

Missing Link

The Fonts tab lists various car-tridges you may have added to your printer. You can choose one of those cartridges to enable the use of its fonts in Windows, and you can also install any printer fonts or new font cartridges.

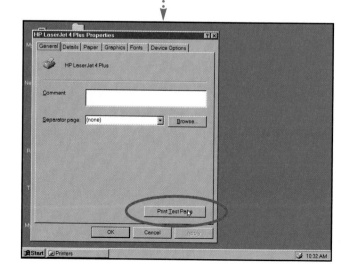

Adding a Printer

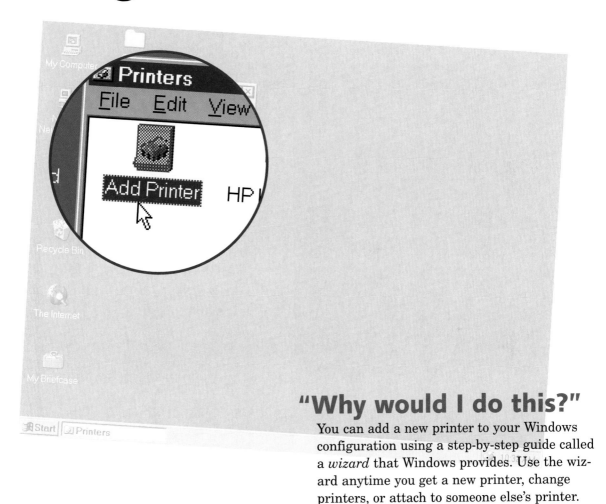

"Why would I do this?"

You can add a new printer to your Windows configuration using a step-by-step guide called a *wizard* that Windows provides. Use the wizard anytime you get a new printer, change printers, or attach to someone else's printer.

1 Open the **Start** menu, choose **Settings**, and then choose **Printers**. In the Printers Folder window, double-click the **Add Printer** icon. The first box of the Add Printer Wizard appears.

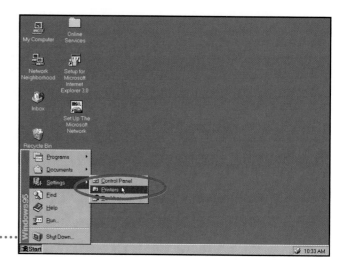

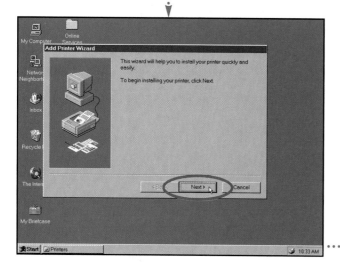

2 Choose the **Next** button to continue with the installation of the new printer. The second Add Printer Wizard box appears.

3 Choose the appropriate option for the connection of the printer (choose **Local Printer** if the printer is physically attached to your computer) and click the **Next** button. A different Add Printer Wizard box appears.

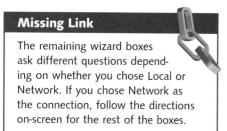

Missing Link

The remaining wizard boxes ask different questions depending on whether you chose Local or Network. If you chose Network as the connection, follow the directions on-screen for the rest of the boxes.

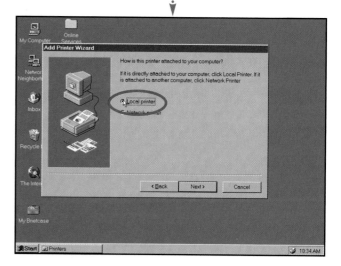

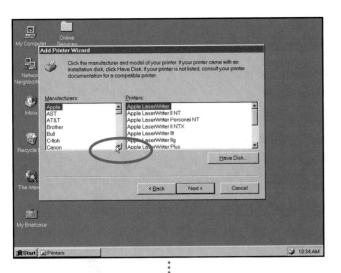

4 Choose the Manufacturers name and then select the printer's name. You can choose the **Have Disk** button and use the manufacturers disk to load the drivers, or you can choose **Next**, and Windows will prompt for the CD or disk to load its own drivers (see step 8). After you load the drivers or choose Next, the Add Printer Wizard box for setting the printer port appears.

5 Choose the appropriate port and select **Next**.

> ### Missing Link
>
> You can cancel this process at any time by clicking the **Cancel** button in any of the wizard dialog boxes. You can also click the **Back** button in a wizard box to go back to the previous dialog box and review or modify your selections.

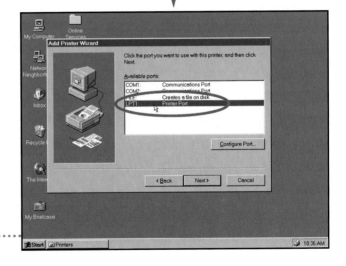

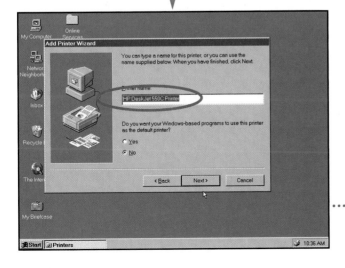

6 Enter a name for the printer, or accept the one Windows has given it. Then choose whether you want the new printer to be the default printer. Click **Next** when you finish.

7 In the final Add Printer Wizard dialog box, choose to print a test page and click the **Finish** button.

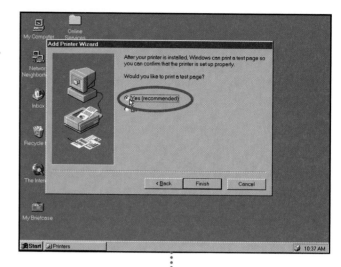

Missing Link

Windows may prompt you to insert a disk or the Windows 95 CD to complete installation of the new printer driver; however, it's more likely that Windows will have the driver stored on your hard disk.

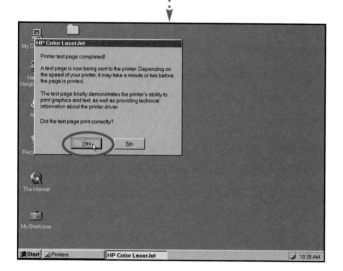

8 Windows displays a message box telling you it printed the test page and asking if it printed successfully. Click **Yes** if it did. Windows then adds the new printer's icon to the Printers folder. ■

PART VI

Personalizing Windows

To make Windows a more comfortable and useful place for you to work, Microsoft has made it easy for you to customize the program. You can move and resize the taskbar, adjust colors and settings, and change other options in Windows to suit your working style. The changes you make to the program affect how you work in your Windows applications as well. If you find you are not satisfied with any of the changes you make in Windows, it's easy to make changes again.

Moving the taskbar to the top or right side of your screen may make it easier for you to work in your applications. You also can hide the taskbar if it gets in your way, and you can resize it to better suit your working style.

One important item you can change in Windows is the date and time on your computer. If the date and time are wrong, saved files display the wrong date, which can cause problems when you are looking for specific files or doing backups. Additionally, many applications enable you to insert the system date into forms, spreadsheets, tables, and so on. If the date on your computer is wrong, inserting the date becomes useless. You can change the system's date and time in the Control Panel.

Another handy option you can change is the screen display. Windows enables you to change the background color on the display, wallpaper (patterns and images you use to decorate your desktop), and the color schemes used for application windows and dialog boxes. You can even set up one of Windows' screen savers to run automatically. (A *screen saver* is a pattern that moves across your screen so the monitor does not burn out after a period of time.)

You can change how your mouse works with Windows. For example, you might change the buttons if you are left-handed, slow the double-click speed, change the appearance of the pointer, and so on. Because you often use the mouse with Windows and Windows applications, you want to be comfortable with the mouse and its workings.

Finally, Windows enables you to add or remove applications from the Start menu to make it more convenient for the way you work. You can, for instance, add a program you use often to the top of the Start menu, and you can add any applications you want to the Programs menu.

Windows makes it easy for you to customize the desktop and other settings so you are more comfortable with your working environment. This part shows you how to customize Windows.

Showing and Hiding the Taskbar

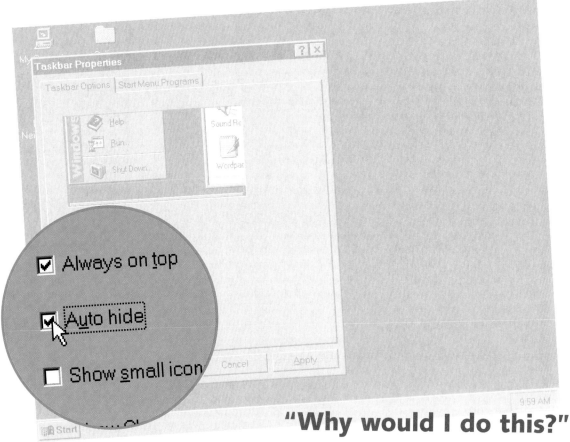

"Why would I do this?"

Windows' default is to show the taskbar at all times on the desktop. You can, however, hide the taskbar so you have more room on the desktop for other windows, folders, and programs. If you hide the taskbar, it disappears while you are working in a window and then reappears when you move the mouse to the bottom of the screen.

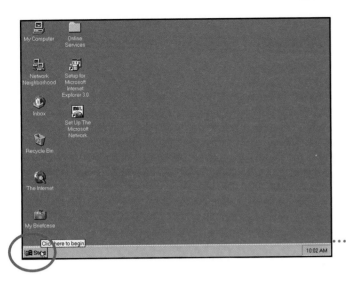

1 Click the **Start** button on the taskbar. The Start menu appears.

2 Choose the **Settings** command, and then choose **Taskbar** from the secondary menu. The Taskbar Properties dialog box appears.

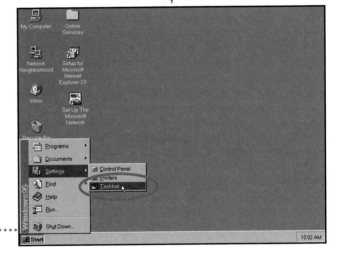

3 Click the **Taskbar Options** tab to display it, if it is not already showing.

127

4 In the Taskbar Options tab, click the **Auto Hide** check box. A check mark appears, indicating that the option is active. If you click the box again, the check mark disappears, and the option becomes deactivated. Click the **OK** button to accept the changes you've made to the Taskbar Options tab. The window closes, and the taskbar disappears.

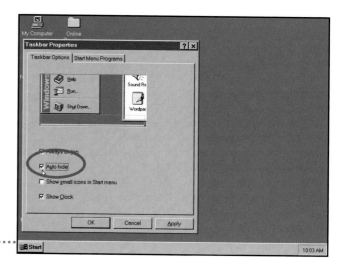

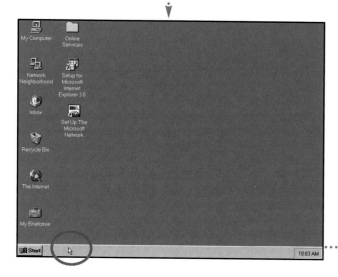

5 To show the taskbar while working, move the mouse to the bottom of the screen. The taskbar appears so you can choose applications or documents.

6 Move the mouse away from the bottom of the screen, and the taskbar disappears again. ■

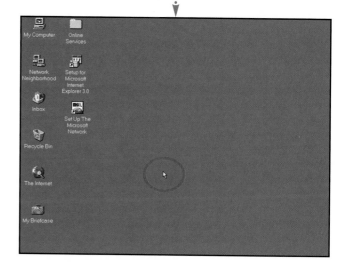

Puzzled?

If you would prefer to show the taskbar at all times, open the **Start** menu and choose the **Settings** command. From the secondary menu, choose the **Taskbar** command. In the **Taskbar Options** tab, click the **Auto Hide** option to remove the check mark. Then click **OK** to accept the change and close the dialog box.

Moving and Resizing the Taskbar

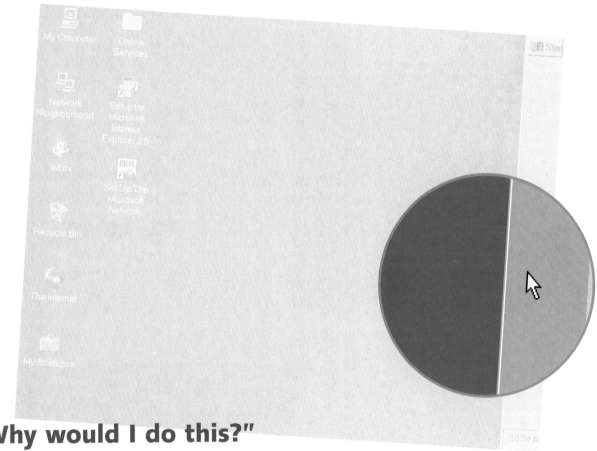

"Why would I do this?"

Windows enables you to move the taskbar to the top, left, or right of the screen so the desktop is more comfortable for your working style. Try moving the taskbar to various areas on the screen, and then choose the area you like best.

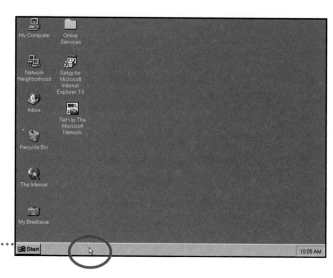

1 Position the mouse pointer anywhere on the taskbar except on a button or the time.

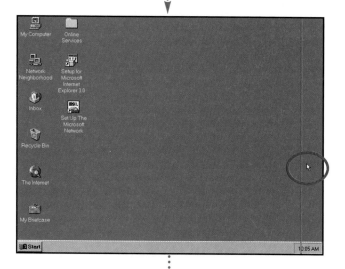

2 Press and hold the left mouse button and drag the taskbar up and to the right. The taskbar's border moves with the mouse; when you release the mouse button, the taskbar jumps to the new location.

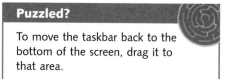

Puzzled?

To move the taskbar back to the bottom of the screen, drag it to that area.

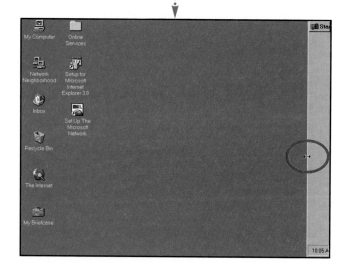

3 To resize the taskbar, position the mouse pointer on one of the taskbar's borders. When you see the double-headed arrow, drag the arrow to resize the taskbar. ■

Starting an Application When You Start Windows

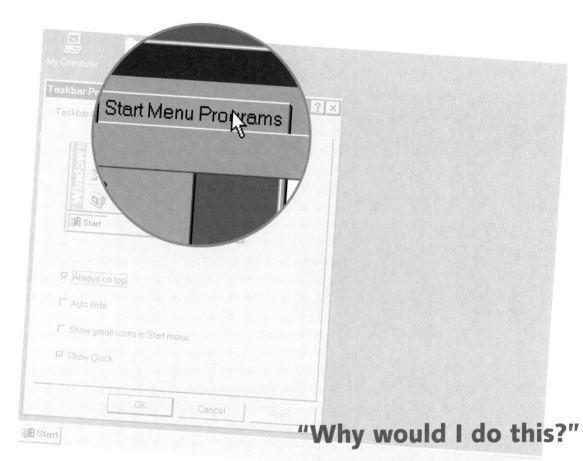

"Why would I do this?"

Windows enables you to start one or more programs with Windows when you turn your computer on. Applications you might want to open automatically are those you use every day or any you use first thing each day. Opening applications with Windows is a shortcut to opening the program after Windows loads.

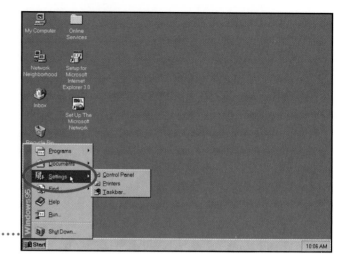

1 Open the **Start** menu and choose **Settings**. Then choose **Taskbar** from the secondary menu to open the Taskbar Properties window.

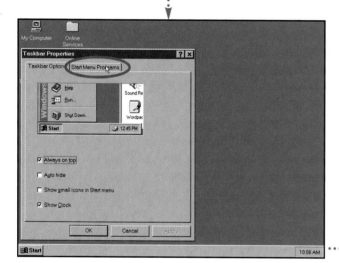

2 Click the **Start Menu Programs** tab. In the Customize Start Menu portion of the window, you can add or remove program names from the Start, Programs menu. Click **Add**, and the Create Shortcut dialog box appears.

3 Click the **Browse** button to open the Browse window. Click the **Look In** drop-down arrow to display the drop-down list, and then choose the folder that contains the program you want to open when Windows starts. The list box displays the contents of the folder.

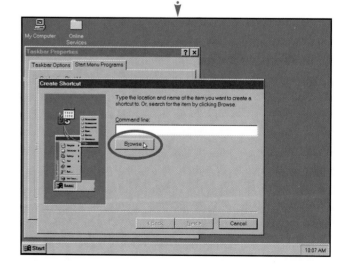

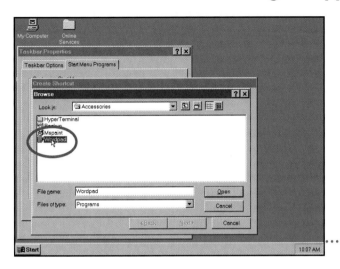

4 Double-click the program you want to start with Windows. In this case, choose **WordPad** from the Program Files\Accessories folder on your hard drive. The Browse dialog box closes, and the command line for the program you selected appears in the Create Shortcut dialog box.

5 Click the **Next** button to display the Select Program Folder dialog box. Then double-click the **StartUp** folder to display the Select a Title for the Program dialog box.

Puzzled?

To remove an icon from the StartUp window, click the **Remove** button in the Start Menu Programs tab of the Taskbar Properties dialog box. In the Remove Shortcuts/Folders dialog box, choose the item you want to remove and click the **Remove** button. Close the Remove Shortcuts/ Folders dialog box, and then click **OK**.

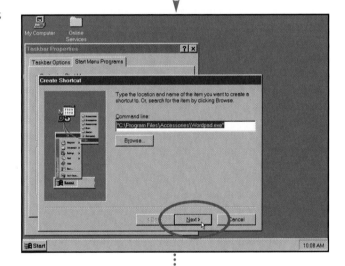

6 Enter a title to place in the StartUp menu or use the one Windows suggests. Then click **Finish**. If Windows asks you to choose an icon, click one and click **Finish**. Click **OK** in the Taskbar Properties dialog box to close it and return to the desktop. ■

133

Opening the Control Panel

"Why would I do this?"

The Control Panel contains settings you can use to modify your Windows environment. You can open the Control Panel from the My Computer window or from the Start menu. This task shows you how to open the Control Panel window so that you can modify common settings.

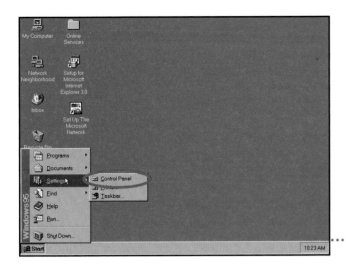

1 Open the **Start** menu and choose the **Settings** command. From the secondary menu, choose **Control Panel**. The Control Panel window opens.

2 Alternatively, you can open the My Computer window by double-clicking the **My Computer** icon on the desktop Then double-click the **Control Panel** folder to open the Control Panel window.

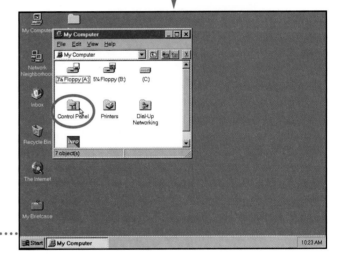

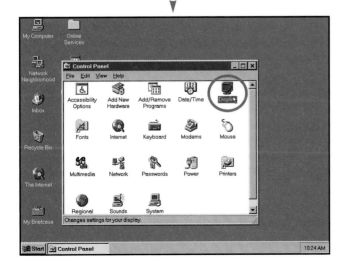

3 You can open any file in the Control Panel window by double-clicking the file's icon.

To close the Control Panel, click the **Close** (X) button in the title bar. ■

51

Changing the System Date and Time

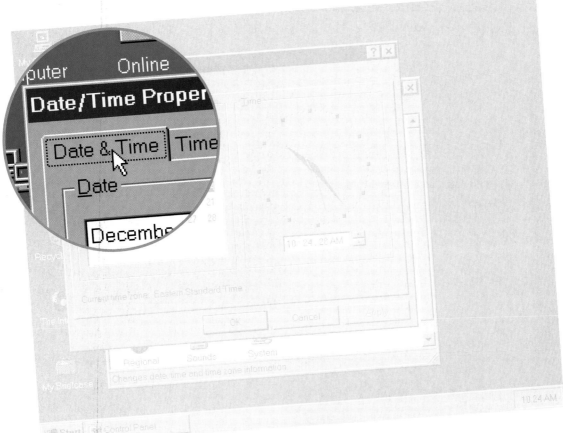

"Why would I do this?"

Your computer places a time and date stamp on every file you save, identifying it for use later. If your system clock is wrong, this feature is not useful. Change your system's date and time if your computer displays the wrong date or time in the taskbar.

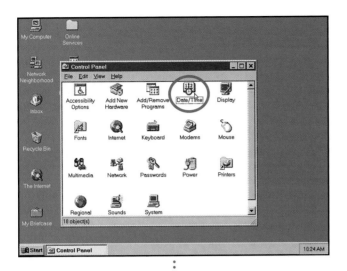

1 Open the Control Panel window and double-click the **Date/Time** icon. The Date/Time Properties dialog box appears. If it is not already showing, click the **Date & Time** tab.

Missing Link

You can also display the Date/Time Properties dialog box by double-clicking the time area of the taskbar.

2 Click the correct date on the calendar to change the date. If the month is wrong, click the down arrow to display the drop-down list and select the correct month. If the year is incorrect, type the correct one in the appropriate text box or use the up and down arrows to adjust the year.

Puzzled?

If the date is wrong the next time you start your computer, you may have a dead battery that you need to replace. If you need help, check the computer's documentation.

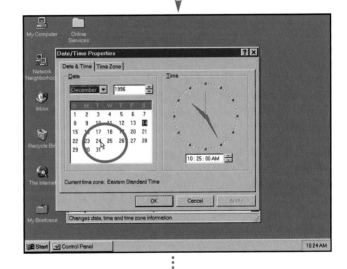

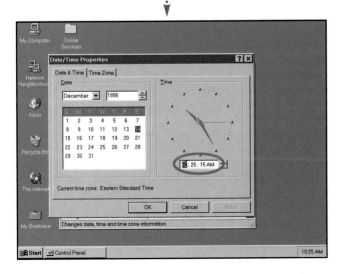

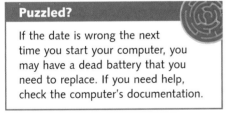

3 In the Time area, use the up and down arrows to adjust the time. Or, select the current time, delete it, and enter the correct time. If you type the time yourself, make sure you use the same format (hour:minutes:seconds and AM or PM). Choose **Apply**, and then click **OK** to accept the changes and close the dialog box. ■

Customizing the Desktop's Background

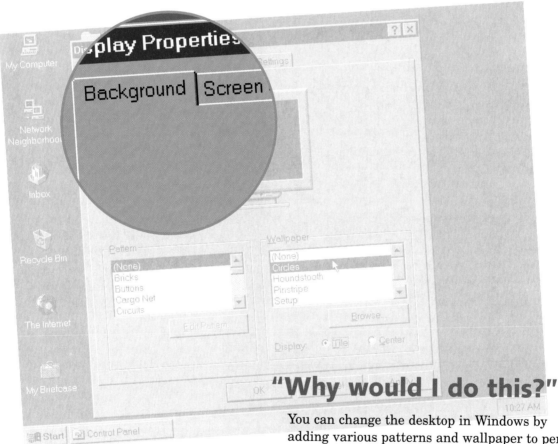

"Why would I do this?"

You can change the desktop in Windows by adding various patterns and wallpaper to personalize your working area or make it more enjoyable. Windows offers paisley, tulip, waffle, and box background patterns (among others), as well as colorful car, honeycomb, square, and zigzag wallpaper patterns, and more. Choose any of these as a background for the desktop, or choose not to use any if you want a calmer effect.

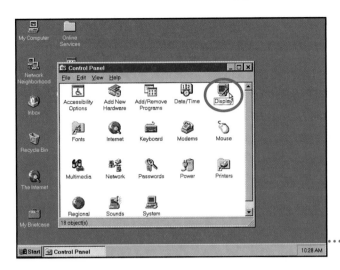

1 Open the **Control Panel** window and double-click the **Display** icon. The Display Properties dialog box appears, with the Background tab showing; if the Background tab is not showing, click it now.

2 To select a pattern, click it in the **Pattern** list; for example, click **Bricks**. The pattern appears on the sample monitor. To have the pattern fill the desktop, choose **Apply** and then click **OK**. Choose **(None)** to remove the pattern.

Missing Link

Using wallpaper and patterns generally slows the speed of your computer and taxes its memory. If your applications seem too slow after you choose wallpaper or patterns, go back into the Display Properties dialog box and choose **(None)**.

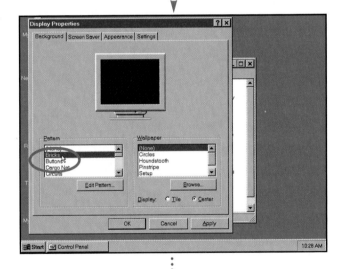

3 To choose a wallpaper, select it from the **Wallpaper** list. The one you select appears on the sample monitor. If you see only one small image in the center of your screen, select the **Tile** option button to fill the screen with the wallpaper image. Choose **(None)** if you prefer no wallpaper. Choose **Apply** and then click **OK** to accept the changes. ■

53

Changing Color Schemes

"Why would I do this?"

Windows enables you to change the color schemes used in Windows and Windows applications to make your work area more comfortable. Lighter colors may, for example, make working in some Windows applications easier on your eyes. On the other hand, you may prefer bright and lively colors.

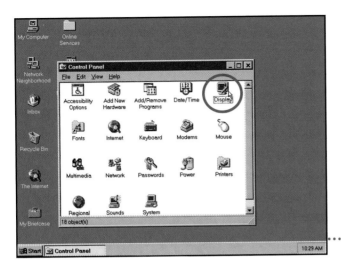

1 Open the **Control Panel** window and double-click the **Display** icon. The Display Properties dialog box appears. Choose the **Appearance** tab.

2 Open the **Scheme** drop-down list by clicking the down arrow. Then choose any of the available color schemes. The color scheme you select appears in the sample box.

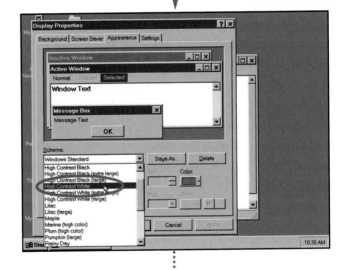

Puzzled?

If you cannot remember the original color scheme, simply click the **Cancel** button to void all changes you've made. This only works before you close the dialog box. After the dialog box is closed, you can change the color scheme only by choosing another one from the Display Properties dialog box.

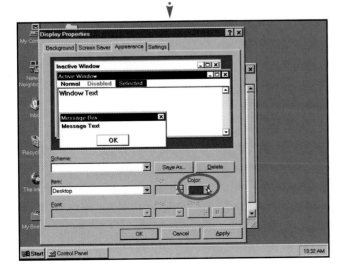

3 After changing the scheme, you can choose a different background color for the desktop from the **Color** list at the bottom of the dialog box. In addition, you can change any item's color by first clicking the item and then selecting a different color from the **Color** list. When you're satisfied with your changes, choose **Apply**, and then click **OK** to accept the changes. Choose **Save As** and enter a name for the new color scheme for later use if you want to. ■

Using a Screen Saver

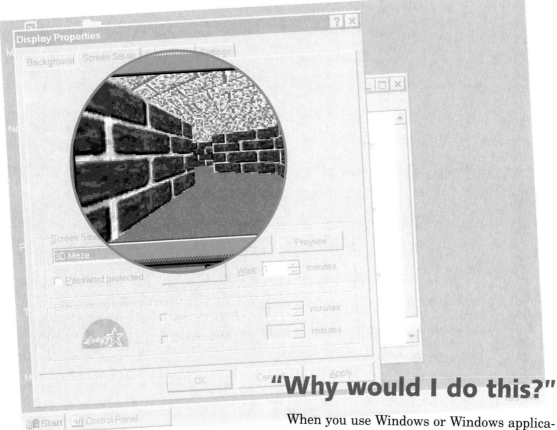

"Why would I do this?"

When you use Windows or Windows applications, the concentration of bright or white colors on your monitor can, over a period of time, burn into your screen (commonly called "burn in"). If that happens, when you turn your computer off or use a DOS program, you still see a "ghost" of the Windows screen on your display. A screen saver (a moving pattern of dark and light colors or images) can help save your screen from this burn-in effect by displaying a pattern whenever your computer is on but is not in use.

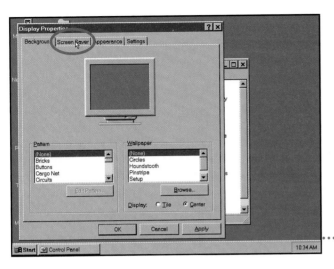

1 Open the **Control Panel** window and double-click the **Display** icon. The Display Properties dialog box appears; choose the **Screen Saver** tab.

2 Click the **Screen Saver** drop-down arrow to display the list of available screen savers. Choose an option, and it appears on the example monitor.

Missing Link

If you want to see the screen saver on the full screen, click the **Preview** button, and Windows displays the entire screen with the saver. Click the mouse button or press the **Spacebar** to return to the dialog box.

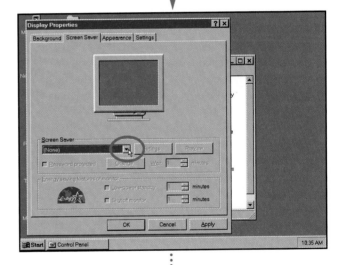

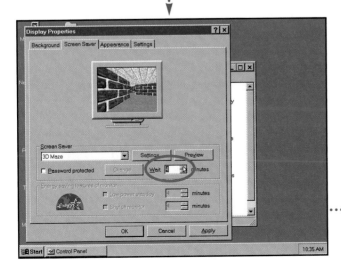

3 In the **Wait** text box, enter the number of minutes you want Windows to wait before it starts the screen saver. If, for example, you enter 10, anytime your keyboard and mouse are inactive for 10 minutes, Windows starts the screen saver, which will continue until you move your mouse or hit a key.

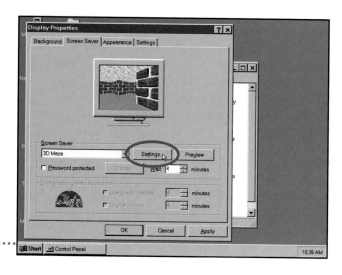

4 With any screen saver selected, choose the **Settings** button to display the Setup dialog box. Each screen saver's setup dialog box is different. Experiment with the settings, and then click **OK** to return to the Display Properties dialog box.

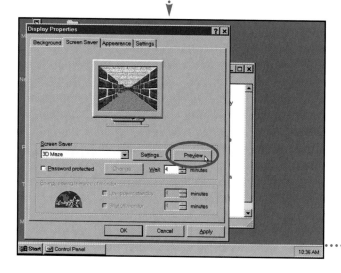

5 Click the **Preview** button to see the changes. Windows displays the entire screen with the screen saver. Click the mouse button or press the **Spacebar** to return to the dialog box.

6 When you are satisfied with the changes to the screen saver, click **OK** in the Display Properties dialog box. ■

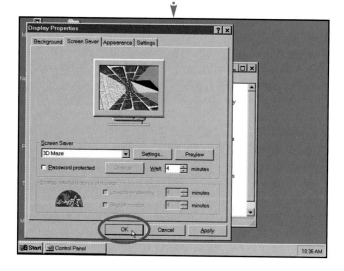

Adjusting the Mouse

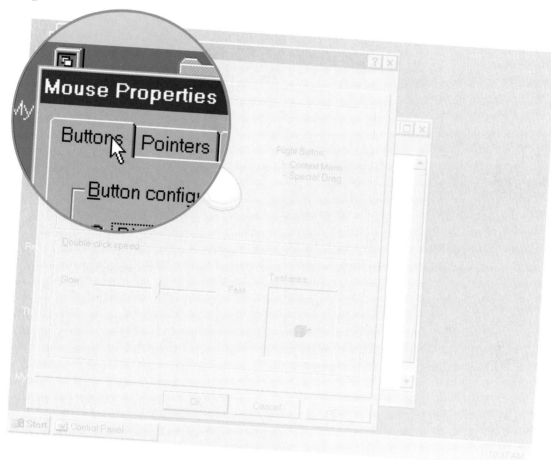

"Why would I do this?"

You can adjust the mouse buttons and double-click speed to make using the mouse more comfortable for you. Say, for example, you are left-handed; switching the left and right mouse buttons can make your work much easier. Likewise, if you are having trouble getting the double-click right, you can change the double-click speed on the mouse.

1 Open the **Control Panel** window and double-click the **Mouse** icon. The Mouse Properties dialog box appears. Choose the **Buttons** tab.

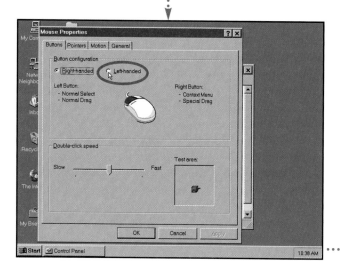

2 If you want to switch the mouse buttons, select the **Left-handed** option button in the Button Configuration area.

3 To change the double-click speed, drag the lever between Slow and Fast. Then test the double-click speed by double-clicking in the Test box. When you double-click correctly, a jack-in-the-box pops out. Double-click again, and Jack goes back into the box.

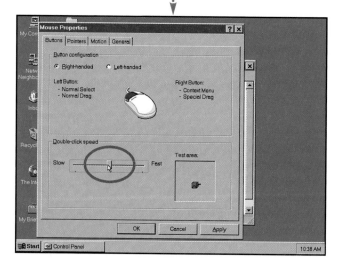

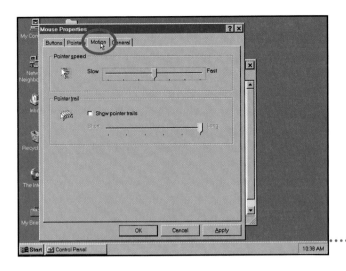

4 Choose the **Motion** tab to change the pointer speed or to leave a mouse trail. You may, for example, want to slow your pointer speed down so you can easily find your mouse on-screen when you move it quickly. Adjust the two options by dragging the lever between Slow and Fast for Pointer Speed and by dragging the lever between Short and Long after checking the Show Pointer Trails option.

5 In the General tab, you can change the mouse that Windows is set up to use. You would change the mouse named in this tab only if you wanted to use a new or different mouse for your computer. To change the mouse, click the **Change** button and follow the directions on-screen.

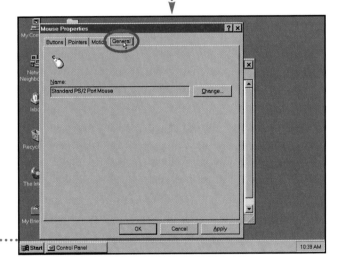

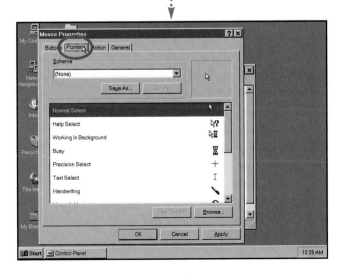

6 In the Pointers tab, you can change the appearance of a pointer. Select the pointer you want to change and click **Browse**. In the Browse dialog box, choose a different file name to apply to the pointer. In the **Scheme** drop-down list, choose Animated Hourglasses if you want to use an hourglass pointer that moves as it displays. When you finish changing the mouse settings, click **OK** to accept the changes and close the dialog box. (Click **Cancel** if you do not want to save the changes.) ■

Changing the Start Menu

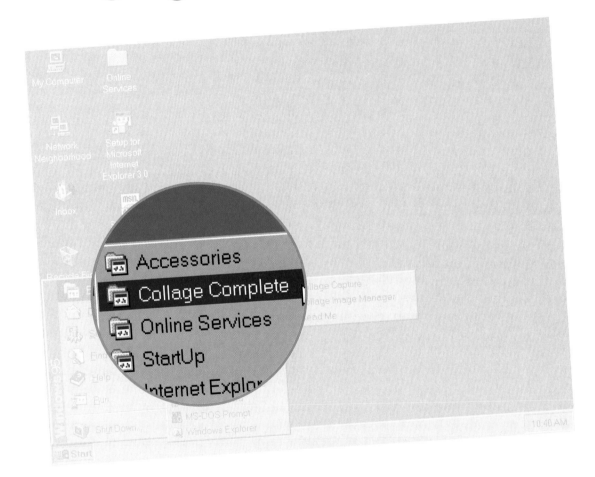

"Why would I do this?"

You can add programs to the Start menu to make it more convenient to use. For example, you may want to add programs that you use often to the Start menu so that you can access them more quickly.

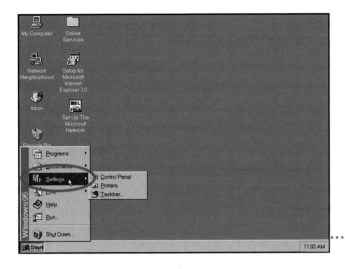

1 Open the **Start** menu and choose the **Settings** command. Then choose the **Taskbar** command from the secondary menu. The Taskbar Properties dialog box appears.

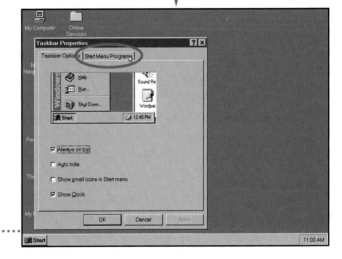

2 Choose the **Start Menu Programs** tab.

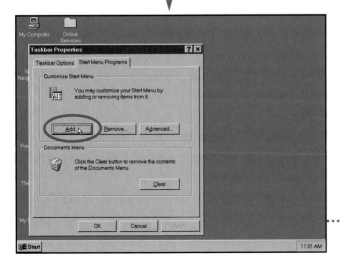

3 To add a program to the Start menu, click **Add**. In the Create Shortcut dialog box, enter the Command line for the program you want to add. Click **Next**, and the Select Program Folder dialog box appears.

Puzzled?

If you don't know the command line, click the **Browse** button, and then select the directory and program name from the Browse dialog box.

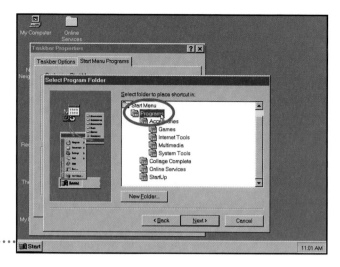

4 Choose the folder in which you want to place the program. Then click **Next**, and the Select a Title for the Program box appears.

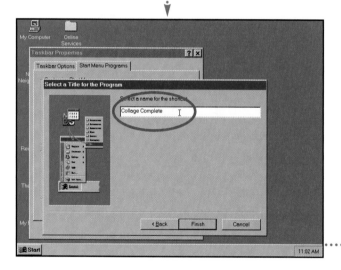

5 Enter a name in the text box or accept the one Windows displays. Click the **Finish** button to put the change into effect.

6 Open the **Start** menu and choose **Programs**. The added program now appears in the Programs menu. ■

Puzzled?

If you want to remove a program from the Start menu, go back into the **Settings** menu and choose **Taskbar**. In the Start Menu Programs tab, choose **Remove** and select the program from the list. Then choose **Remove**, choose **Close**, and click **OK** to close the Taskbar Properties dialog box.

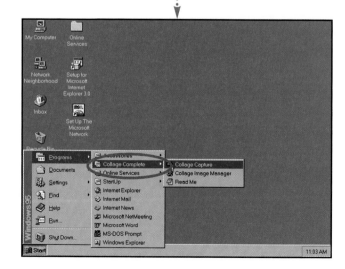

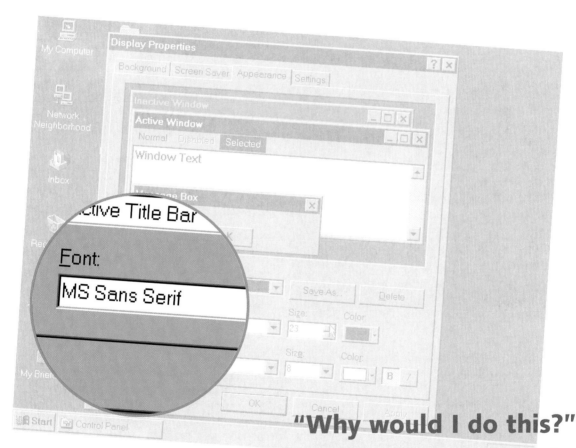

Viewing and Changing Display Fonts

"Why would I do this?"

You can change the fonts that Windows displays in dialog boxes and windows to any font in your system. Changing the display font personalizes your screen. In addition, changing the typeface, size, or color of the font may make it easier on your eyes when you have to look at the screen for long periods of time.

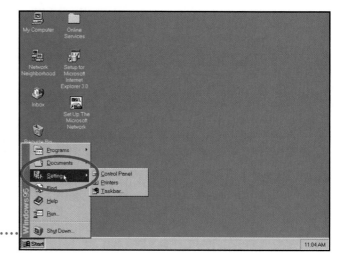

1 Open the **Start** menu and choose **Settings**. From the secondary menu, choose **Control Panel**. The Control Panel window opens. The Control Panel enables you to customize Windows (to change settings controlling the way Windows works). You can, alternatively, open the Control Panel by double-clicking its icon in the My Computer window.

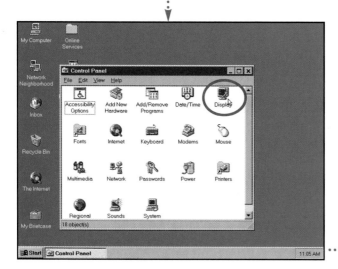

2 In the Control Panel, double-click the **Display** icon to open the Display window. The Display Properties dialog box appears, with four tabs that offer options for changing your display: Background, Screen Saver, Appearance, and Settings.

3 Choose the **Appearance** tab. The Appearance tab contains options for changing fonts, color scheme, and so on. Click an area in the sample screen and then change the item.

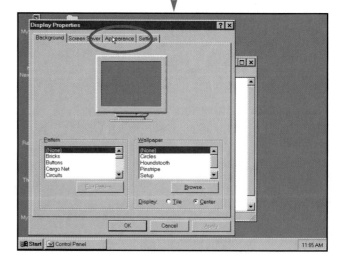

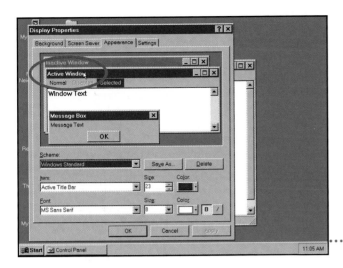

4 In the sample screen, click the title bar with the words Active Window. The item changes to Active Title Bar, and the default scheme, font, color, and other settings appear below the sample screen. Any changes you make apply to the selected item.

5 Click the **Fonts** drop-down arrow to display the list of available fonts. Select the font you want; for example, select **Times New Roman**. Notice the changes in the selected item.

> **Puzzled?**
>
> Any changes you make in this dialog box can easily be reversed; simply choose **Cancel** to close the Display Properties dialog box.

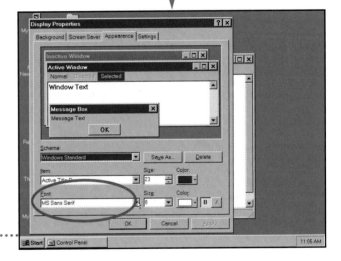

6 Click the **Size** drop-down arrow to display a list of available sizes. Select the size you want. Note you can also change the color of the font or the background by choosing an option from the **Color** drop-down list. If you like the changes, click the **Save As** button and name the color scheme. (Windows saves the font type and size with the color scheme.) When you're happy with your changes, click **OK**. ■

PART VII

Sharing Data with Windows

WINDOWS MAKES IT EASY for you to open several applications at once and switch between them using the taskbar. Furthermore, you can open and view two or more applications on-screen at one time so you can easily compare or share the information between the applications.

One of the biggest advantages of using Windows and Windows applications is that you can easily and efficiently share data—text, figures, pictures, lists, and so on—between the applications. Whether you are working with word processing documents or spreadsheets, databases or drawing programs, you can share the data in all of your Windows applications.

Windows provides several methods of sharing data between applications: copying, moving, linking, and embedding. Suppose you create a spreadsheet of quarterly sales and you want to use the figures in a report to your boss. You can use any of the sharing methods to accomplish this task.

You can select and copy the data in the spreadsheet application and then switch to the word processing application that holds the text of the report. Paste the data and format it like you would any other text. The original data remains in the spreadsheet program for later use, and it also appears in the report.

You can move the text from the spreadsheet program to the report if you no longer need it in the original program or file. Selecting and cutting the data removes it from the spreadsheet program and places it on the Clipboard (an area in Windows set aside for holding copied or cut material). Material stays on the Clipboard until you cut or copy something else; you can paste material from the Clipboard over and over again. From there, you can paste it to the report in the word processing program, for example.

You can create a link between the spreadsheet and the report that updates the data automatically whenever you change it in the spreadsheet program. When you use *OLE* (Object Linking and Embedding), you can be sure your work is always current and accurate.

Windows applications that support OLE enable you to tie together documents between two applications (called the source and the destination). You create the data in the source, such as the spreadsheet program. You then create a link between the source and the destination—the report in the word processing program, for example. Then, whenever you change the data in the source, it is automatically updated in the destination. So when you make a change to the spreadsheet, it is automatically updated in the report.

OLE also enables you to share data by *embedding* information instead of linking. When you embed data, you create the data within the destination application using the source application. In the report, for example, you choose the spot in which you want to insert spreadsheet data. Through the Edit menu of the word processing application, you then open the spreadsheet program as an "object" and create the spreadsheet within the destination application. When you complete the spreadsheet, you close the source application and the spreadsheet becomes embedded in the word processing document. If you need to update the data, you can double-click the spreadsheet in the word processing program, and the spreadsheet application opens, ready for editing.

Switching Between Applications

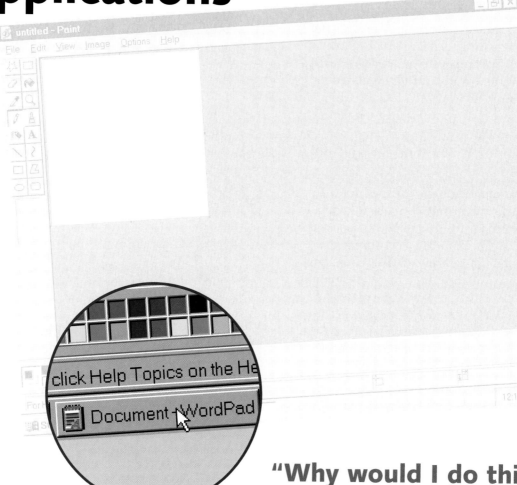

"Why would I do this?"

You switch between applications so you can complete your work efficiently and effectively. Switching between applications enables you to share and compare data so you can update and complete your work faster and easier.

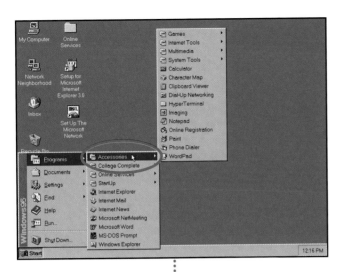

1 From the **Start** menu, open your word processing program. If you do not have a word processing program installed, you can select the **Accessories** folder and click **WordPad**. Then, in the program window, click the **Minimize** button. Notice the program's icon on the taskbar.

Missing Link

The number of programs you can have open at any one time depends on the amount of RAM (random-access memory) in your system.

2 Then open a spreadsheet or another program. For example, open the **Start** menu, select **Accessories**, and choose **Paint**. Windows displays the second program on-screen, and a button representing it appears in the taskbar.

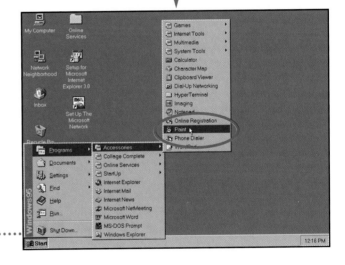

3 To switch back to the word processor, click the program's button on the taskbar. Windows enlarges the first program window and displays it on-screen. ■

Puzzled?

Instead of switching between programs using the taskbar, you can arrange the open application windows on-screen. Right-click any empty spot on the taskbar and choose the **Tile Horizontally** or **Tile Vertically** command from the menu that appears.

157

TASK 59

Viewing the Clipboard

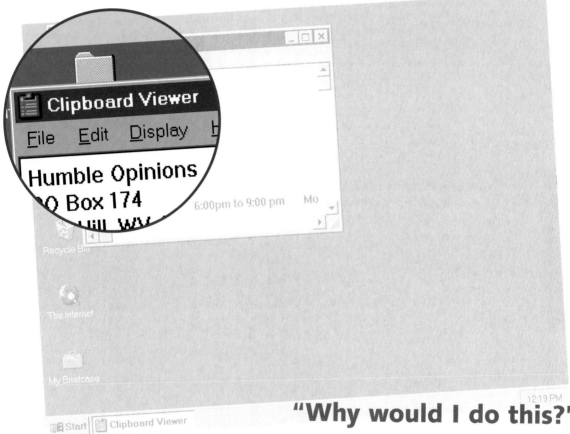

"Why would I do this?"

You can use the Clipboard Viewer to view, edit, and save material you've cut or copied to the Clipboard. Whenever you choose to cut or copy material in any Windows program, that material is placed on the Clipboard. You can then paste the material to another location, document, or application. Whenever you cut or copy something else, the material that's currently on the Clipboard is replaced. However, you can use the Clipboard Viewer to save that material for use at another time.

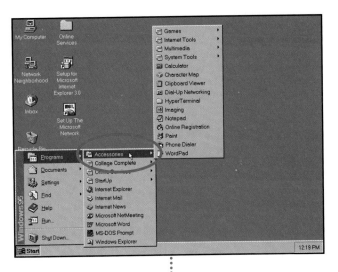

1 Click the **Start** button and choose **Programs** From the secondary menu, choose **Accessories** and then choose **Clipboard Viewer**. The Viewer's icon looks like a clipboard.

2 If you have cut or copied material during the current session, the Clipboard Viewer window appears with that material. To save the material in a file to itself, choose **File**, **Save As**. In the Save As dialog box, enter a name for the file in the **File Name** text box. Clipboard files are saved with .CLP extensions in the C:\WINDOWS\DESKTOP folder. Click **OK** to save the file. You can view the Clipboard file at any time by choosing **File**, **Open** in the Clipboard Viewer and choosing the saved file name. Choose **File**, **Exit** to close the Clipboard Viewer. ■

Missing Link

If the Clipboard Viewer option is not on the Accessories menu, you must install it. To do so, open the **Control Panel**, double-click the **Add/Remove Programs** icon, choose the **Windows Setup** tab, and double-click **Accessories** in the **Components** list. The Accessories dialog box appears. In the Accessories Components list, choose **Clipboard Viewer** and then click **OK**. Click **OK** to add the Clipboard Viewer. Then follow the on-screen directives.

Copying Data Between Applications

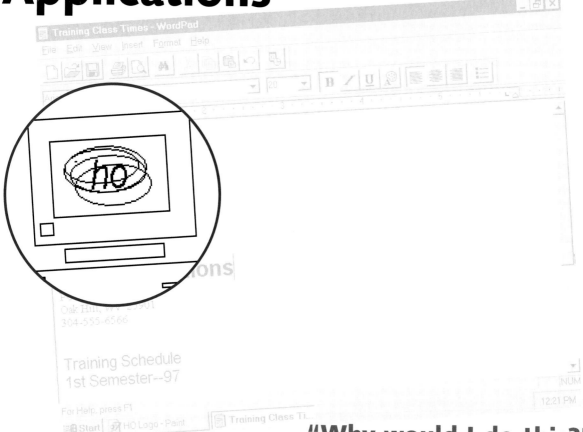

"Why would I do this?"

You can copy data from a document in one application and paste it into another document in another application to save time typing. In addition to text, you can copy spreadsheets, figures, charts, clip art, and so on. Using copied text and graphics saves you time in your work and makes your documents look attractive and professional.

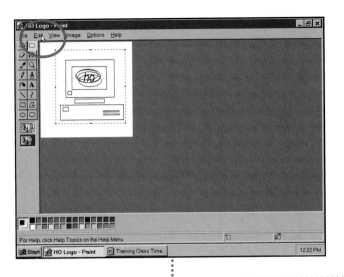

1 Open any two Windows applications and enter data—numbers, text, sound, or graphics—into one of the applications. Select that data. Then open the **Edit** menu and choose the **Copy** command. Windows copies the data to the Clipboard.

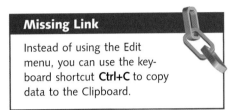

Missing Link

Instead of using the Edit menu, you can use the keyboard shortcut **Ctrl+C** to copy data to the Clipboard.

2 Click the taskbar button representing the program you want to switch to. Windows displays the application.

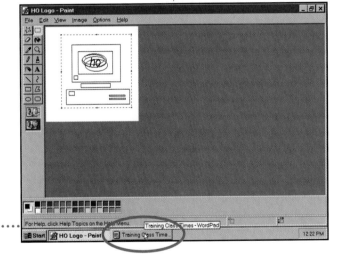

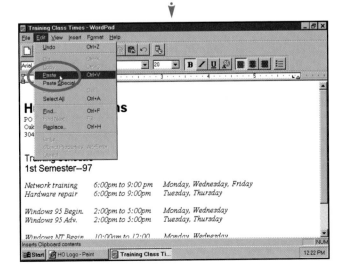

3 Position the insertion point in the document, open the **Edit** menu, and choose the **Paste** command. (Or you can press the shortcut key **Ctrl+V**.) The data is pasted into the document. ■

TASK 61

Moving Data Between Applications

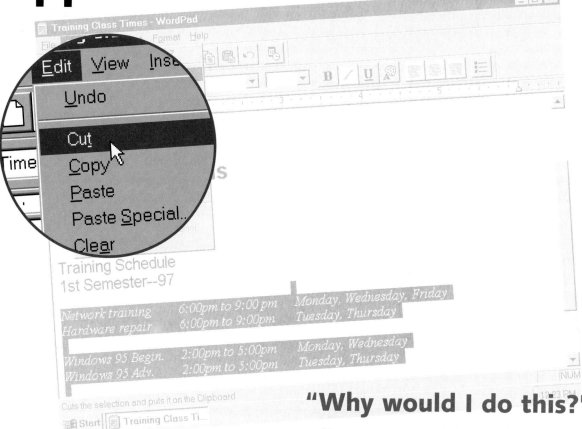

"Why would I do this?"

You can move, or cut, information from one application to another so you can represent it in the proper format. When you move or cut text or a graphic, it no longer exists in the original location. Suppose, for example, you entered tomorrow's schedule in WordPad; however, as you work you want to use an alarm like the one in the Calendar accessory to notify you when it's time for your first meeting. You can cut the schedule from WordPad and move it to the Notepad accessory where you can set the alarm.

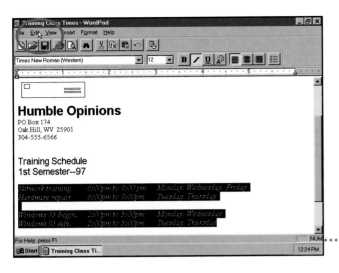

1 Open any two Windows applications, enter data into one of the applications, and select that data. Then open the **Edit** menu and select the **Cut** command.

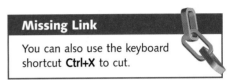

Missing Link

You can also use the keyboard shortcut **Ctrl+X** to cut.

2 Click the taskbar button representing the program you want to switch to. Windows displays the application.

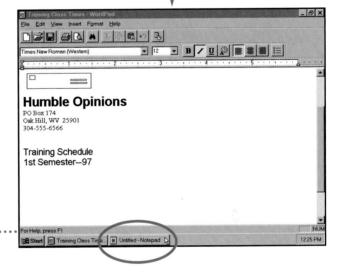

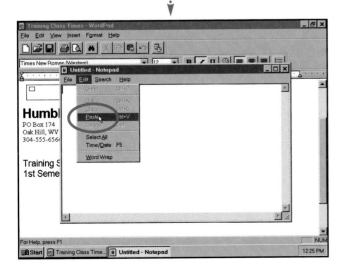

3 Position the insertion point in the document, open the **Edit** menu, and choose the **Paste** command. (Or you can press the shortcut key **Ctrl+V**.) The data is pasted into the document. ■

Puzzled?

You can undo a paste operation if you change your mind after performing the action. Choose **Edit**, **Undo Paste** to remove the data you just pasted.

TASK 62

Linking Data Between Applications

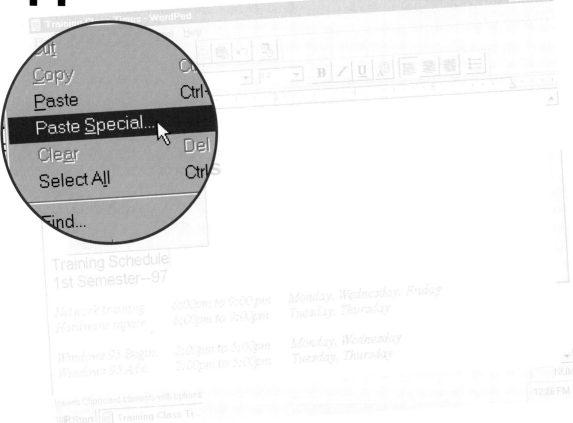

"Why would I do this?"

You might link data between applications if you want the data to be updated automatically when you edit or add to the source document. Linking data saves you time because you only have to edit the information once; Windows OLE then updates any linked files for you.

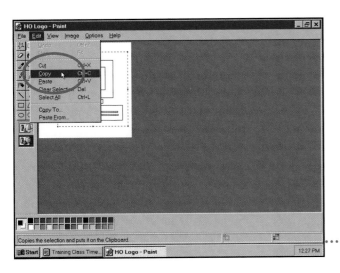

1 In the source document, select the data you want to link. Then open the **Edit** menu and choose the **Copy** command. Windows copies the selected data to the Clipboard.

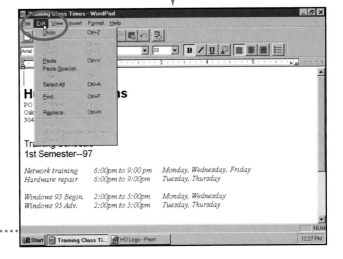

2 If the destination document is already open, click its taskbar button to switch to it; if the destination document is not already open, open the application and document now. Then position the insertion point where you want the linked data to go, open the **Edit** menu, and choose the **Paste Special** command. The Paste Special dialog box appears.

3 Select the **Paste Link** option button, and then select the format you want to paste from the **As** list box. The available formats depend on the type of data you're pasting (in other words, they'll change). You can, for example, choose to paste a picture as a Metafile or a Bitmap. Choose a Bitmap file if you have a dot-matrix printer, for example, because the structure of a bitmap object works best with that printer. Click **OK**, and Windows inserts the data with a link between the destination and the source files. ■

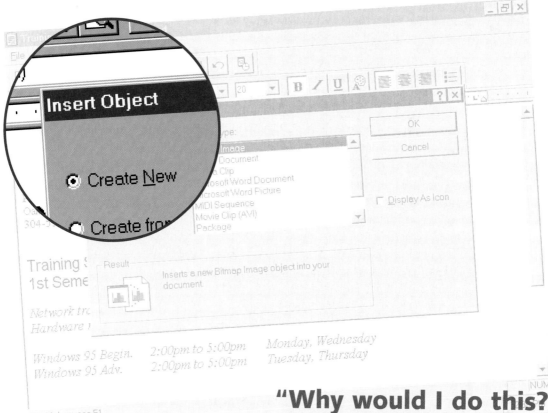

Embedding an Object

"Why would I do this?"

You can use embedding when you do not already have a source document for the data you want to share. Creating a source document within the destination document makes it easy for you to edit data quickly and efficiently. For example, suppose you are working in a word processing document and want to add a spreadsheet that will change weekly to incorporate new figures. Embed the spreadsheet so that when you need to change the figures, you can simply double-click the spreadsheet within the report and make the changes.

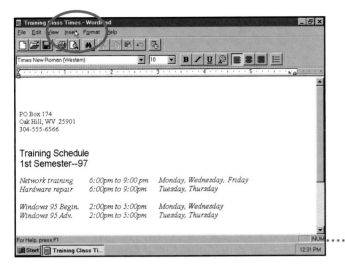

1 In the destination document, position the insertion point where you want the embedded object to go. Then open the **Insert** menu, and choose the **Object** command. The Object dialog box appears. Not all applications' Insert Object dialog boxes look the same, but all are similar. From the list of object types, choose the application in which you want to create the data. Then click **OK**, and the application window opens.

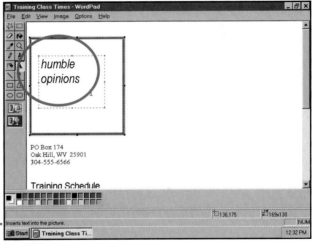

2 Enter the data as you normally would in that application.

> ### Puzzled?
> Not all Windows applications support Object Linking and Embedding. If you cannot find an Insert Object command, check the application's documentation to see if the application supports OLE.

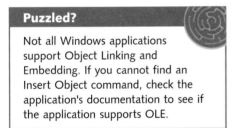

3 When you are done, open the **File** menu. Look for an **Update** command and choose it. Then look for an **Exit and Return to Document** command. (Sometimes the two commands are combined, and sometimes they don't exist at all; just click outside of the source document to return to the destination document.) Windows closes the application and embeds the data into the destination document. ■

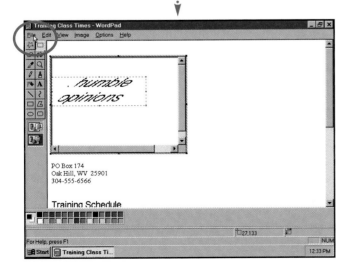

> ### Puzzled?
> Anytime you want to edit the embedded object, just double-click it. The source application opens, and you can edit the object.

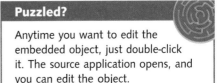

PART VIII

Using Windows Accessories

WINDOWS PROVIDES SEVERAL ACCESSORIES, or applications, you can use to help you in your work. These accessories are not full-blown applications, but they are useful for specific jobs in the Windows environment. Among the accessories are a calculator, games, a painting program, a word processor, and Internet applications. The Internet applications are discussed in Part 9, "Using Internet Explorer."

Included with Windows are several games you can play on the computer. Minesweeper and Solitaire are two games traditionally associated with Windows. Solitaire is the card game we all learned as children, and Minesweeper is a game of chance. Additionally, Windows includes FreeCell and Hearts. FreeCell is a variation of the Solitaire game in which you try to make four stacks of the fifty-two cards in order of rank and suit. You can play the card game called Hearts with the computer or with other people on your network. The object of the game is to get the lowest score.

Windows also provides a simple word processor called WordPad. WordPad enables you to enter and edit text files, such as the AUTOEXEC.BAT or CONFIG.SYS. Furthermore, you can format text in WordPad using various fonts, type sizes, tab settings, and text alignment. You can even insert objects using OLE. WordPad is limited, however, in that it does not check spelling or provide for headers and footers, kerning, and other complex word processing features.

In addition to WordPad, Windows includes a text editor: NotePad. NotePad is a bare-bones word processor you can use to edit basic text files. Many Windows files (such as the help files

and readme files) are in the NotePad format.
You cannot format text in NotePad, but you can
print files, search for specific words or phrases,
and save and open text documents.

Occasionally you may need to insert artwork of
some type into your documents. Windows' Paint
enables you to create and edit drawings, as well
as edit clip art, screen captures, and other
graphic files. Paint is a basic drawing and
painting program that comes in handy for
quickly polishing your artwork.

Finally, you can use any of the Windows
Multimedia tools to play CDs or other media
(such as film clips) and to record and play back
sounds to accompany presentations and so on.

The more you work in Windows, the more occa-
sion you will find to use many of the Windows
accessories. This part shows you how to open
and use the accessories described.

64

Playing Games

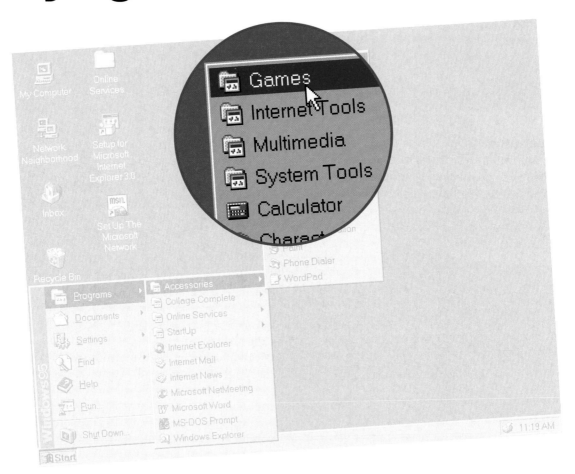

"Why would I do this?"

Windows provides several games you can play to break up your workday with a little entertainment. Use any of the games to fill a lunch hour or coffee break and to ease the tensions of the day. This task shows you how to open the games accessories in Windows.

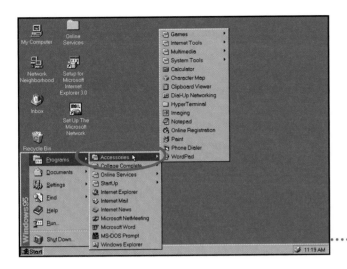

1 Open the **Start** menu and choose **Programs**. Then select the **Accessories** folder and choose the **Games** folder. From the Games menu, click the name of the game you want to open, such as **Solitaire**. The game's window appears.

2 After opening the game, choose the **Help** menu for instructions on how to play the game.

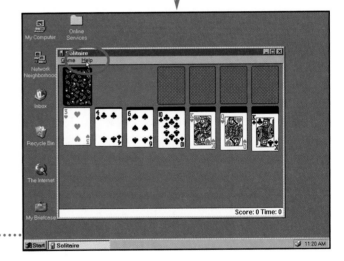

3 To close any game in Windows, click the **Close** (X) button in the title bar. ■

TASK 65

Controlling Multimedia

"Why would I do this?"

You can use various Windows multimedia devices, such as the Sound Recorder or Media Player, to add to the presentations or documents you create in Windows. Use the CD player to listen to audio CDs, view film clips with the Media Player, or record your own sounds and insert the sound files into your documents for clarification or interest.

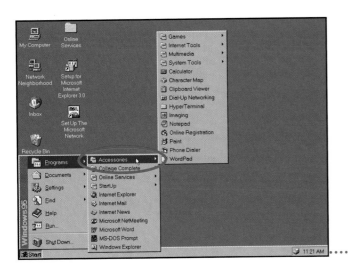

1 To open the Multimedia folder, open the **Start** menu and choose **Programs**. Then choose **Accessories**, **Multimedia**. The secondary menu appears, containing several options.

Missing Link

To get the most from the multimedia features in Windows 95, you need to have a sound card, speakers, and an SVGA monitor installed.

2 Choose the **CD Player** from the Multimedia menu. The CD Player window appears. The CD Player works similarly to a CD player in your stereo. You can choose to play, pause, stop, fast-forward, or rewind the CD in the drive. You can choose the tracks you want to play and arrange them in various orders according to the artist or title (if you are set up to play multiple discs). Click the **Close** button to close the CD Player window.

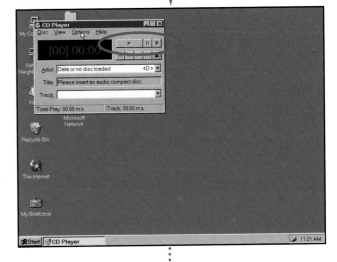

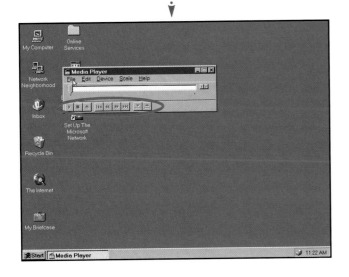

3 Choose **Start**, **Programs**, **Accessories**, **Multimedia**, and **Media Player** from the Multimedia menu to play audio, video, and animation files. You can use the controls at the bottom of the Player to play, pause, stop, fast-forward, rewind, and otherwise control the playback. To close the Media Player, click the **Close** button. ■

Writing and Editing in WordPad

"Why would I do this?"

Use WordPad to edit text files, such as your AUTOEXEC.BAT (a configuration file), or to quickly create formatted text, such as notes, memos, fax sheets, and so on. WordPad saves files in Word 6 for Windows format by default, but you can choose to save in a text-only format when editing configuration files.

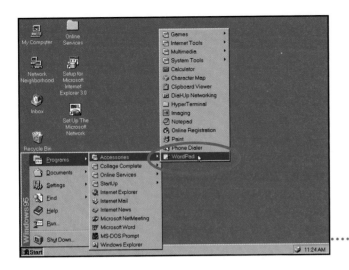

1 Open the **Start** menu, choose **Programs**, select the **Accessories** folder, and choose **WordPad**. The WordPad window appears with a toolbar, format bar, ruler, and status bar ready to help you with your work.

2 Click the **Maximize** button to enlarge the WordPad window and make it easier to work in. The blinking cursor in the work area indicates where new text will appear when you type.

Missing Link

To hide any of the screen elements in WordPad, choose the **View** menu and click the tool you want to hide. A check mark indicates the tool is showing; no check mark indicates it is hidden.

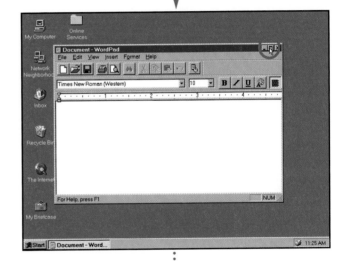

3 Type your name and press **Enter**. Pressing Enter creates a new paragraph by moving the blinking cursor down one line.

Puzzled?

If you want to type paragraphs of text, you do not need to press Enter at the end of a line of text to start a new line. WordPad has an automatic text wrap feature; you press Enter only to start a new paragraph.

4 To change fonts, click the **Font** drop-down arrow on the Format Bar. Scroll to the top of the list and choose **Arial.** All text you enter will be in the Arial font until you choose a different font. (You can also choose the Font command from the Format menu to select a new font.)

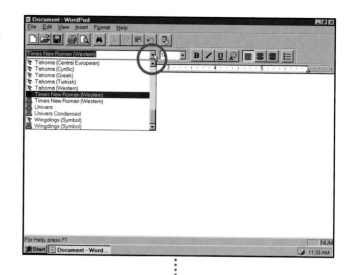

Missing Link

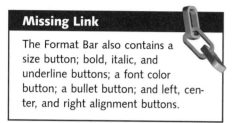

The Format Bar also contains a size button; bold, italic, and underline buttons; a font color button; a bullet button; and left, center, and right alignment buttons.

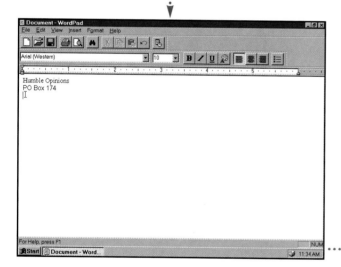

5 Enter your address at the insertion point (the blinking cursor). Press **Enter**. If you make a mistake while typing, press the **Backspace** key to delete one character at a time. Alternatively, you can drag the mouse over any text to highlight the text and then press the **Delete** key to remove the text.

6 To save a file, open the **File** menu and choose the **Save As** command. The File Save As dialog box appears. In the **Save In** list box, choose a drive and/or folder in which to save the document.

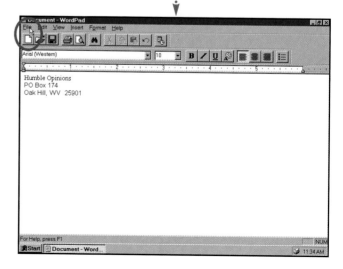

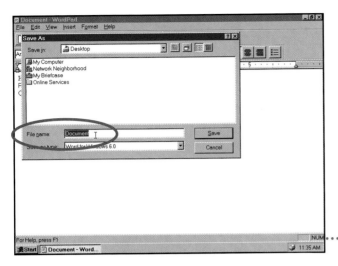

7 In the **File Name** text box, enter a name for the file, such as Document. You can enter a file name that's up to 255 characters, if you want, to describe your document. Click **Save** to save the file.

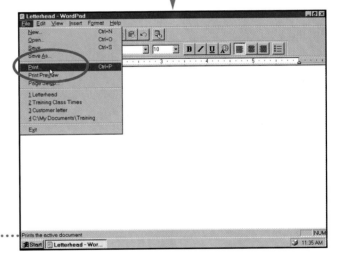

8 To print a document, open the **File** menu and choose the **Print** command. The Print dialog box appears. Choose the **Print Range** and enter the number of copies you want. Then click **OK** or press **Enter** to print the document.

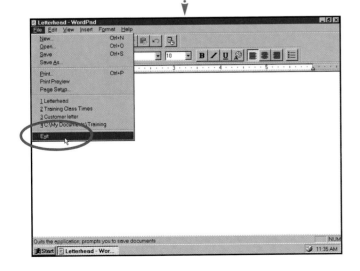

9 To close WordPad, open the **File** menu and choose the **Exit** command, or click the **Close** button in the program's title bar. ■

177

Using Paint

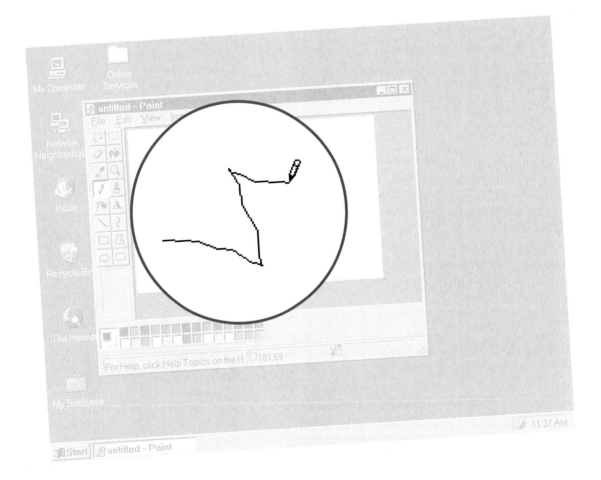

"Why would I do this?"

Use Paint to create art and to edit graphics such as clip art, scanned art, and art files from other programs. You can add lines, shapes, and colors, as well as alter the original components.

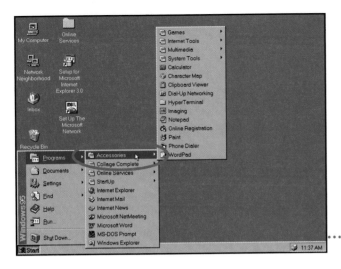

1 Open the **Start** menu, choose **Programs**, and select the **Accessories** folder. From the Accessories menu, choose the **Paint** command. The Paint window opens, with the pencil tool active.

2 Drag the pencil tool around to get the feel for freehand drawing. If at any time you do not like what you've drawn, open the **Edit** menu and choose **Undo.**

Missing Link

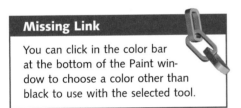

You can click in the color bar at the bottom of the Paint window to choose a color other than black to use with the selected tool.

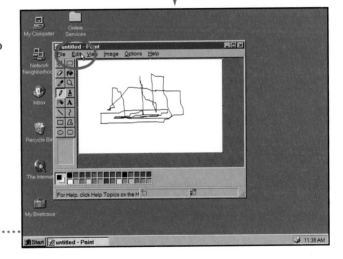

3 On the toolbar, click the rectangle tool. To draw a rectangle in the work area, click the tool at the point you want the top left corner of the rectangle to be, and then drag the tool diagonally down and to the right to create the shape. You can click any tool on the toolbar, and the program displays a description of the tool in the status bar.

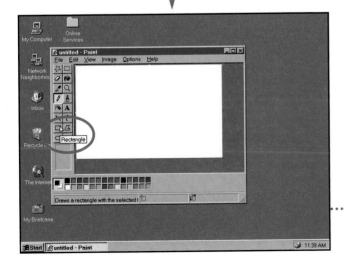

4 Click the Select tool on the toolbar and drag the mouse across part of your drawing. The tool creates a rectangle as you drag, and anything within the rectangle is selected. Press the **Delete** key to remove the selected part of the drawing.

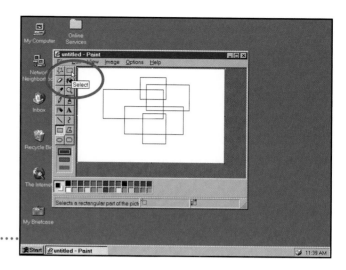

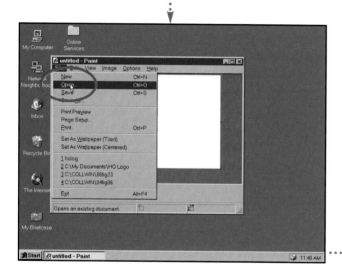

5 To edit a piece of art in Paint, you must first open it. Open the **File** menu and choose **Open**. The Open dialog box appears. In the **Look In** list box, choose your hard drive.

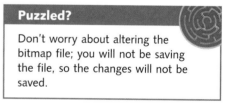

Puzzled?

Don't worry about altering the bitmap file; you will not be saving the file, so the changes will not be saved.

6 In the list of folders and files, choose the **WINDOWS** folder and select the **PIN-STRIPE.BMP** file to open it (or type **C:\WINDOWS\PINSTRIPE.BMP** in the **File Name** text box and click **Open**). Paint displays a dialog box asking if you want to save the changes to the untitled document. Choose **No**. The PINSTRIPE.BMP file is a Windows bitmap file used for wallpaper. The file opens on-screen.

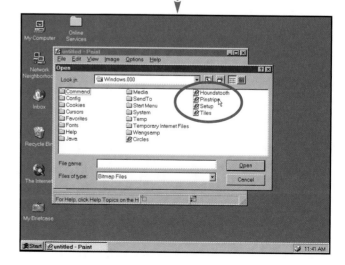

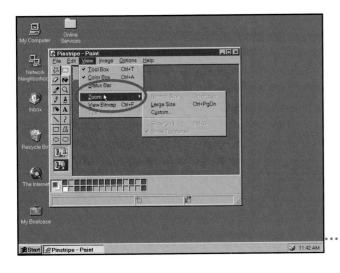

7 Open the **View** menu and choose **Zoom.** From the secondary menu that appears, choose **Large Size.** The art becomes larger. Using the Paint tools, draw and color the art any way you like.

Missing Link

You can click in the color bar at the bottom of the Paint window to choose a color other than black to use with the selected tool.

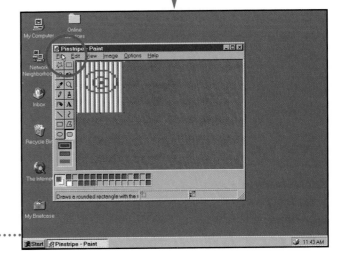

8 When you finish with the drawing, open the **File** menu and choose the **New** command. Paint displays a message asking if you want to save the file. Choose **No** to cancel the changes.

9 To close the Paint application, open the **File** menu and choose **Exit.** ■

PART IX

Using Internet Explorer

68 Setting Up for the Internet

69 Using Internet Explorer

70 Using Internet Mail

71 Using Internet News

PART OF WINDOWS 95 IS MICROSOFT'S Internet Explorer 3.0, a Web browser that offers you complete and convenient browsing of the Internet. As with any browser software, you can use the Internet Explorer to view World Wide Web pages, search for specific topics, download and upload files, and save links to certain Web pages in order to mark them for quick and easy access the next time you connect.

Windows 95 also includes an Internet Mail application you can use to exchange e-mail messages with others who are connected to the Internet. E-mail is quickly becoming the most popular form of communication between friends, family, and especially businesses. Imagine the possibilities: You can contact customers, vendors, employees, managers, and anyone else you work with quickly and successfully—without having to play phone tag or deal with voice mail or long periods of holding.

With Internet Mail, you can view, read, respond to, and sort messages. You also can store, delete, forward, and otherwise manage e-mail messages. And Internet Mail even provides an address book in which you can store e-mail addresses, and to which you can add and delete addresses as your list of contacts expands.

One other Internet application included with Windows 95 is Internet News. With more than 15,000 newsgroups on the Internet, Internet News enables you to exchange ideas and information about business, politics, hobbies, and many other interests. UseNet newsgroups (forums in which people exchange ideas on the Internet) enable you to contact others with ideas similar to or completely different from your own. You can pose questions about your new computer, state opinions about the best type of dog to use for hunting grouse, discuss your home decorating ideas, or meet people who write science fiction short stories. There are literally thousands of forums you can search, read through, and visit time and again. Windows' Internet News application enables you to browse through a list of available UseNet groups, search groups for a topic or description, view a topic and related responses that have been posted, and much more.

Naturally, you must have an Internet connection before you can use the Internet Explorer, Internet Mail, or Internet News. Windows makes it easy for you to configure your Internet connection; first, however, you'll need to get an Internet Service Provider (ISP) in your area. An ISP provides you with all of the information— the IP address, subnet mask, host name, and so on—that you need to configure Windows 95 for the Internet.

This part of the book shows you how to configure Internet Explorer and then how to use the three Internet applications: Internet Explorer, Internet Mail, and Internet News.

TASK 68

Setting Up for the Internet

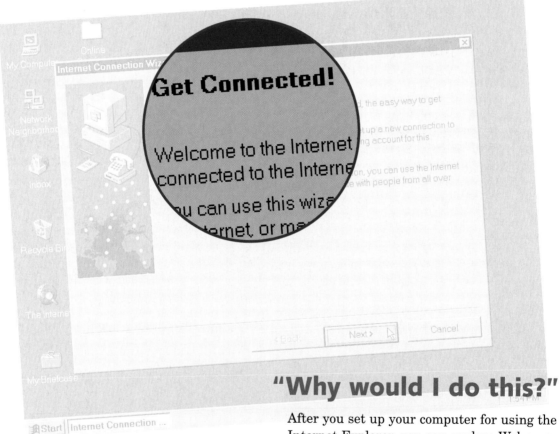

"Why would I do this?"

After you set up your computer for using the Internet Explorer, you can explore Web pages, send and receive e-mail, and access newsgroups on the Internet. Windows makes it easy to set up for using the Internet by providing a wizard that guides you through the steps.

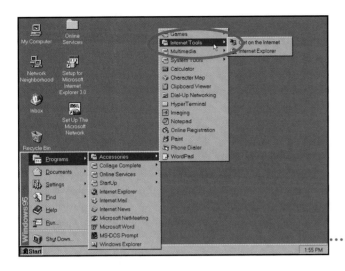

1 Choose **Programs**, **Accessories**, **Internet Tools**, and then select **Get on the Internet** from the submenu. The Internet Connection Wizard appears. Click the **Next** button to start the process.

2 Choose the **Manual** option if you have an account with an ISP and want to set up your computer with addresses and information your ISP has provided. Click the **Next** button to continue setup. (If you do choose Manual, an introductory screen appears; click **Next** to move on.)

Puzzled?

If you do not have an ISP and you want Windows to find an ISP for you, choose **Automatic** and follow the directions on-screen in the wizard dialog boxes that follow.

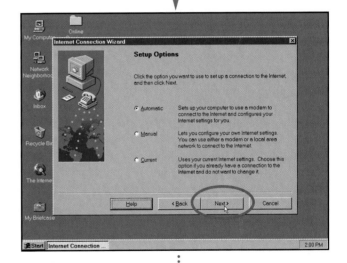

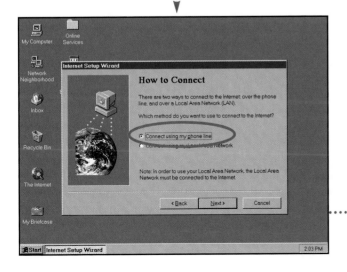

3 The How to Connect wizard box appears. Select the method you'll use to connect to the Internet. You'll most likely use the phone line to connect, so you'll choose the first option; however, if you're a member of a network, you'll choose the second (LAN) option instead. These instructions assume you're using a phone line. Click **Next**.

185

4 The wizard next asks if you want to use Internet Mail. Choose **Yes** and click the **Next** button. If you do not set up Internet Mail, you won't be able to send or receive e-mail messages over the Internet using Windows' Internet mail application.

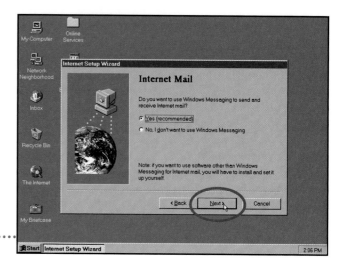

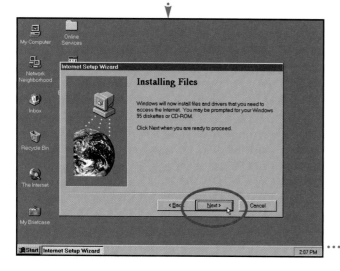

5 The Installing Files wizard dialog box appears. Click **Next** to continue the process. Windows may prompt you for your Windows CD-ROM; if so, insert the disk and click **OK** to continue.

6 When Windows is done copying files, it displays the Service Provider Information wizard dialog box. Enter the name of your ISP and click **Next**.

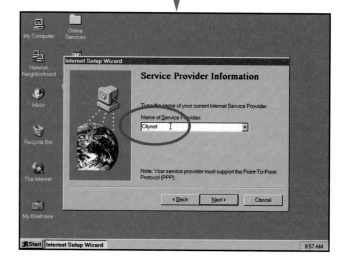

7 In the Phone Number wizard dialog box, enter the area code (if applicable) and the phone number of your ISP. Choose the country code if it's not the U.S., and then click the **Next** button.

8 In the User Name and Password wizard dialog box, enter the user name and password assigned to you by your ISP. Notice the password appears as asterisks instead of characters to protect your privacy. When you finish, click **Next**.

9 In the IP Address dialog box, choose the appropriate response and click the **Next** button. Your ISP may provide your IP address automatically through a special server, called a DHCP server; however, make sure you check with the ISP first before choosing that option. Generally, you enter an IP address (which your ISP assigns you) in this wizard box.

187

10 In the DNS Server Address dialog box, enter the number(s) or name(s) for the DNS server(s) your ISP uses. (This information, as well as all other information you use in the wizard, should have been provided by your ISP.) Click **Next**.

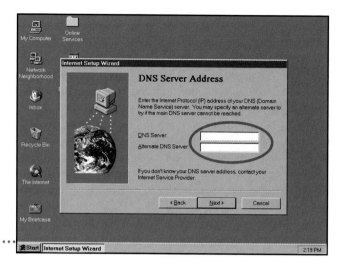

11 If you're configuring for Internet Mail, enter your e-mail address and your ISP's Internet mail server in the Internet Mail wizard dialog box. Then click the **Next** button.

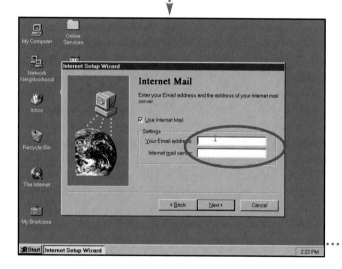

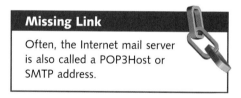

Missing Link

Often, the Internet mail server is also called a POP3Host or SMTP address.

12 The Complete Configuration wizard dialog box appears to let you know that setup is complete. Click the **Finish** button. From now on, when you click The Internet icon on the desktop, the connection you just created will appear (as described in the next task). ■

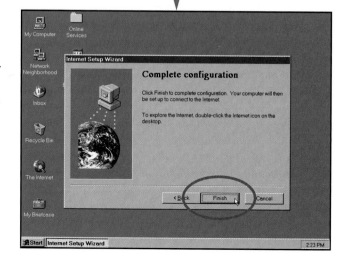

Using Internet Explorer

"Why would I do this?"

You must specify a phone number, user name, and password before you can use Internet Explorer to connect to the Internet. Task 68 walks you through creating a connection with your ISP. After you connect to the Internet, you can explore the World Wide Web. Some things you can do on the Web include shopping for books, researching your business competition, finding people, getting technical support for software, and much, much more. If you have trouble with any of the settings, contact your ISP for technical help.

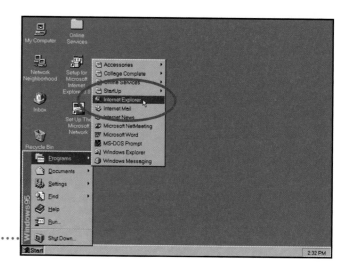

1 To open Internet Explorer, double-click the icon on your desktop labeled **The Internet**; alternatively, you can choose **Start**, **Programs**, **Internet Explorer**.

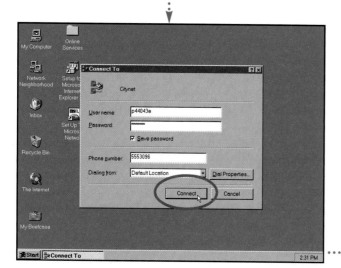

2 The Connect To dialog box appears. You can make any necessary changes to the phone number or dialing properties before you connect to the Internet. Click the **Connect** button to continue, and Windows dials the number and connects to your ISP.

3 The Internet Explorer window appears. Microsoft programs its home page to be your first stop on the information highway. You can always click the **Stop** tool button to cancel the home page before it is completely loaded; then you can choose the Web page you want to visit instead.

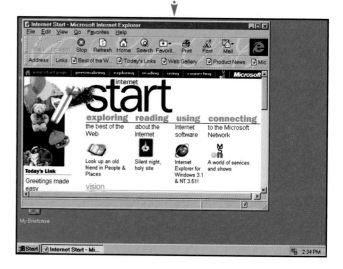

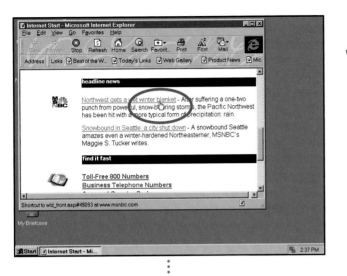

4 Click any underlined text (called a *link* or *hyperlink*) on a Web page to view more information related to that text. If the mouse pointer appears as a pointing hand, that means you're pointing to a link.

Missing Link

You can use the scroll bars or press the **Page Up** and **Page Down** keys to move around in any Web page.

5 Click the **Back** button in the toolbar to go to the previous page you visited. From there, you can click the **Forward** button to move forward through the pages you've already visited. To go back to the Microsoft home page at any time, click the **Home** button in the toolbar. To find a specific topic, click the **Search** button and enter the word or phrase for which you want to search.

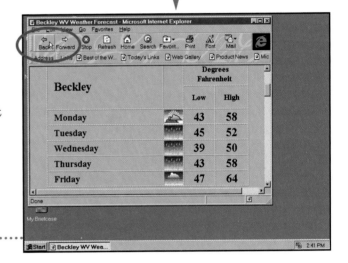

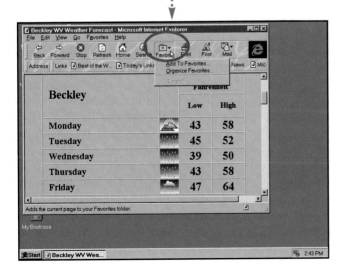

6 If you find a Web page you like that you think you might want to visit again, click the **Favorites** button on the toolbar, choose **Add To Favorites**, and enter the name you want to appear on your Favorites menu. Windows records the address and will go to that address any-time you click the name on the menu.

When you're done with Internet Explorer, choose **File**, **Close**. In the Disconnect dialog box, choose **Yes** to disconnect. If you choose No, you remain online and can use Internet Mail or Internet News. ■

Using Internet Mail

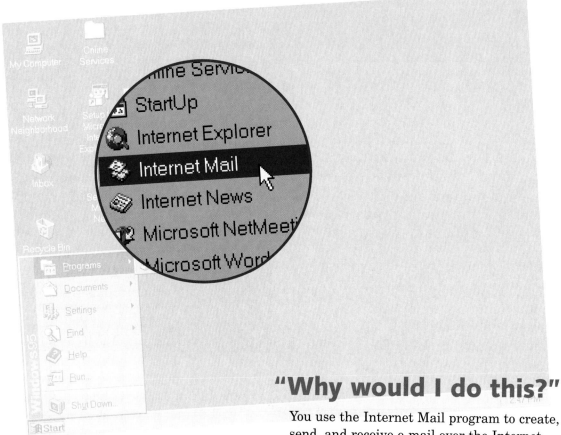

"Why would I do this?"

You use the Internet Mail program to create, send, and receive e-mail over the Internet. You can send messages to colleagues, clients, friends, and family, and you can read and reply to messages others send you. You can also send files—such as reports, spreadsheets, pictures, and so on—as files attached to your messages.

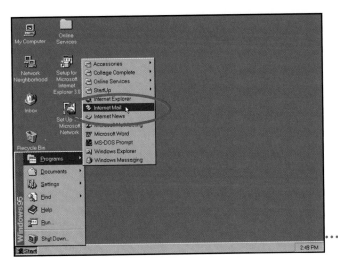

1 To open the Internet Mail application, choose **Start**, **Programs**, **Internet Mail**. Your computer must already be configured for use over the Internet; see Task 68.

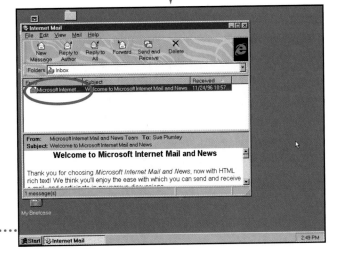

2 The Internet Mail window appears. You can read the Microsoft welcome letter, if you want, in the bottom pane of the window. (Click the **Maximize** button to enlarge the window, if necessary.)

3 To create a new message, click the **New Message** button on the toolbar or choose **Mail**, **New Message**. Enter the address of the person to whom you're sending the mail in the **To** text box; if you want to send a carbon copy of the message, enter the address of the recipient in the **Cc:** field. Enter a topic in the **Subject** field, and then you can enter your message in the text area.

193

4 Click the **Send** button or choose **File**, **Send Message**. If you're not connected to the Internet, Windows places the message in the Outbox and displays a dialog box notifying you of this; Windows will send the message the next time you connect to the Internet.

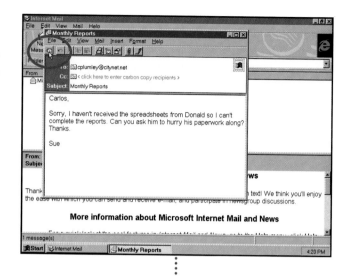

Missing Link

To attach a file to your message, choose **Insert**, **File Attachment**. Choose the file you want to attach and click the **Attach** button.

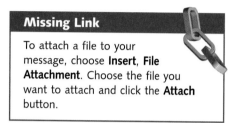

5 To connect to the Internet from the Internet Mail application, click the **Send and Receive** button on the toolbar or choose **Mail**, **Send and Receive**. The Connect To dialog box appears. Make any appropriate changes in the dialog box, and then click **OK**.

6 Windows connects to your ISP mail server and sends your message. It also receives any messages in your post office box. When it's finished, Windows remains connected to the Internet.

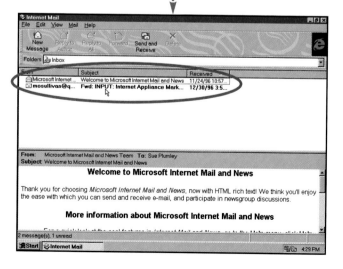

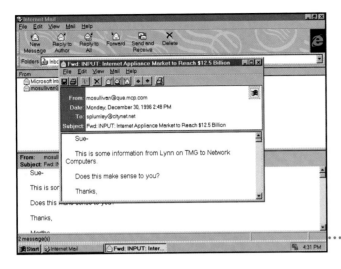

7 To open a message, double-click the message in the Internet Mail window. Scroll through the lower pane if necessary to read all of the message.

8 To reply to a message, click the **Reply** button or choose **Mail**, **Reply to Author**. The text of the original message is inserted into the reply pane, and the blinking cursor appears at the top of the message window. Enter the message and click the **Send** button.

To print an open message, choose **File**, **Print** and then click **OK.**

To save an open message, choose **File**, **Save As**. Then assign the message a file name and location and click **Save**.

To add an address to your address book, choose **File**, **Add to Address Book**.

To delete a message, choose **File**, **Delete**.

To close a message, choose **File**, **Close**.

To change various options about messages, choose **Mail**, **Options**.

To close Internet Mail, choose **File**, **Close**. If Windows prompts you to disconnect from the network, choose **Yes**. ■

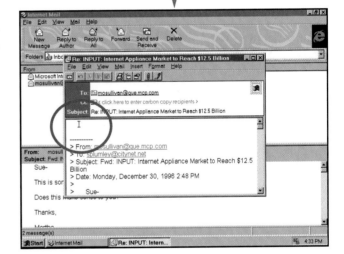

TASK 71

Using Internet News

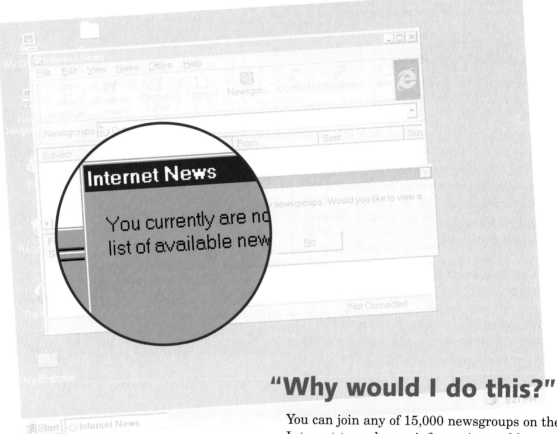

"Why would I do this?"

You can join any of 15,000 newsgroups on the Internet to exchange information and learn about hobbies, businesses, pets, computers, people of different walks of life, and more. With Internet News, you can browse (look at various groups and see what they're about), lurk (read and observe, but not participate), and join in with any of these newsgroups.

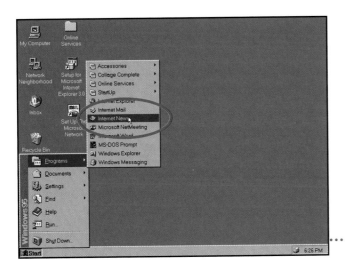

1 To open the Internet News application, choose **Start**, **Programs**, and **Internet News**.

2 The Internet News window appears. If you've not subscribed to a newsgroup, a dialog box appears asking if you want to view a list of the available newsgroups. Choose **Yes** to display the Connect To dialog box, and then click **OK** to connect to the Internet.

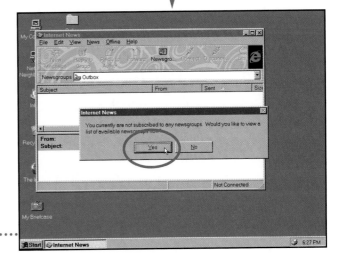

3 After connecting, Internet News downloads a list of newsgroups. The application may display the News Logon dialog box, in which you enter your account and password for the news server. Click **OK** when you're done. If the server doesn't respond to your user name and password, remove all text from the News Logon dialog box and click **OK**. (Some servers don't require any logon.)

197

4 Scroll through the list to find a newsgroup you want to view or join. Select it and click the **Go To** button to view the topics and messages in that group.

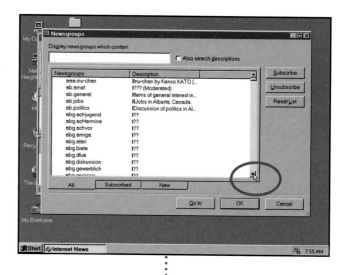

Missing Link

You can search for a specific word—such as "computers" or "banjo," for example—by entering the word in the **Display Newsgroups Which Contain** text box.

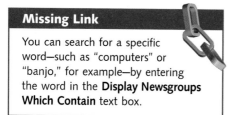

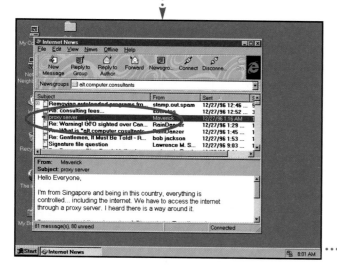

5 Select a topic you want to read about in the upper pane of the Newsgroup window, and the message appears in the bottom pane. Scroll to read the message, or select and read another message.

6 To reply to a message, click either the **Reply to Group** button on the toolbar or the **Reply to Author** button. The Reply window appears with the original message already in place within the reply. Enter your message, and then click the **Post Message** button on the toolbar or choose **File**, **Post Message**.

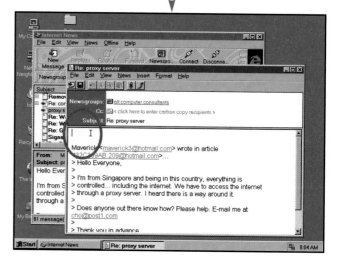

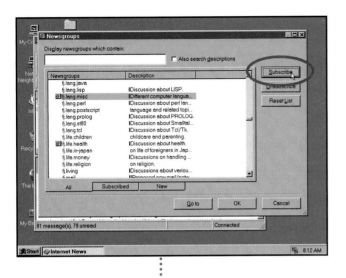

7 To subscribe to a group while in the group's list, choose **News**, **Subscribe to This Group**. You also can subscribe to a group from the Newsgroups window within the list of groups, by selecting any group and clicking the **Subscribe** button. Windows places a small newspaper icon beside the newsgroup to indicate you're a member of that group.

8 To download the messages in any group so you can read and reply to them offline, select the message and then choose **Offline**, **Mark Message for Download**. You can also mark an entire thread (all messages related to one subject), or you can mark all messages for download.

To return to the list of newsgroups, click the **Newsgroup** button on the toolbar.

To print any message, select it in the Internet News window and choose **File**, **Print**.

To save a message, select it and choose **File**, **Save Message**. Then assign the message a location on your hard drive and click **OK**.

To disconnect from the Internet at any time, choose **File**, **Disconnect**.

To change the order of the displayed messages, choose **View**, **Sort By**, and then select **Subject**, **From**, **Sent**, or **Size**. By default, the messages are sorted by time and date the messages were sent.

To exit Internet News, choose **File**, **Close**. ■

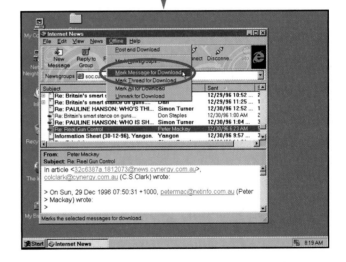

Missing Link

To disconnect from the Internet if Windows doesn't prompt you to disconnect, you can open the My Computer window and double-click the **Dial-Up Networking** icon. Select your connection in the Dial-Up Networking window and choose **File**, **Disconnect**.

PART X

Maintaining Windows 95

WINDOWS PROVIDES MANY ADVANCED FEATURES that enable you to control your applications and files. This last part of the book introduces four advanced techniques you may find useful while working in Windows: installing new applications, installing new hardware devices, defragmenting a disk, and scanning a disk for damage.

You'll likely need to install Windows applications—such as Microsoft Office, Lotus 1-2-3, CorelDRAW!, and so on—now that you're familiar with Windows. No matter what type of Windows application you choose to install, the basic procedure remains the same, and it's fairly simple and straightforward. This part explains the fundamentals of installing a Windows application.

Windows makes installing new hardware—such as modems, printers, mice, and so on—relatively easy with hardware wizards. A *wizard* is a series of dialog boxes that Windows displays; the dialog boxes give you information and ask questions about the hardware devices. If you do not know details about your hardware, you can instruct Windows to detect the hardware. Windows then tries to figure out what kind of hardware is attached to your computer, and if it can, it configures the hardware for use without further input from you. If by chance, Windows cannot correctly detect the hardware, you must enter the information manually by checking the documentation that came with the specific hardware you are installing.

Another useful feature included with Windows is the Defragmenter. When you save many files to a hard or floppy disk, your computer stores the files in pieces. Your computer stores some pieces together consecutively. However, your computer divides and stores other files in pieces on different areas of the disk; these files are said to be *fragmented*. Fragmented files do not normally hurt anything. However, when you access a fragmented file, it takes longer for the computer to find all of the pieces. The Windows Defragmenter helps to speed access to files on your computer by consolidating files and storing them in contiguous units.

Another problem Windows can help you with is disk damage. Windows provides a program called ScanDisk that checks your hard disk for damage and can often retrieve data from damaged areas of the disk. In addition to scanning the disk and reporting damage, ScanDisk generates a log of its results so you can view details of the various areas scanned.

Installing Windows Applications

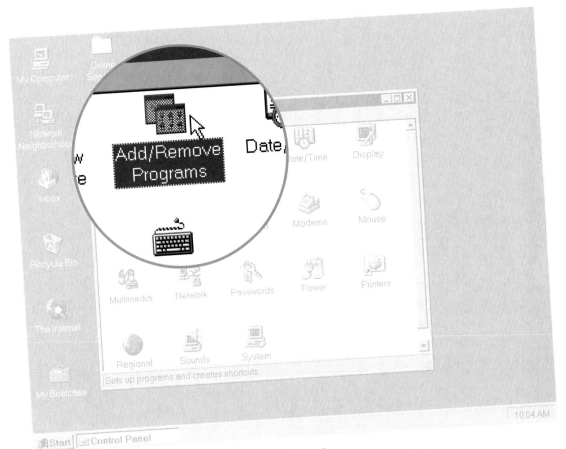

"Why would I do this?"

To make the most of Windows power, you install and use the applications you need to perform your work. You can install word processing, database, or spreadsheet programs—or any other Windows programs—to Windows 95 using the Add/Remove Programs Properties dialog box and the application's installation disks.

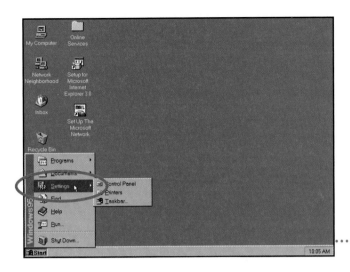

1 Insert the first installation or setup disk in your A or B floppy drive. Open the **Start** menu and choose the **Settings** command. Then choose the **Control Panel** from the secondary menu. The Control Panel window appears.

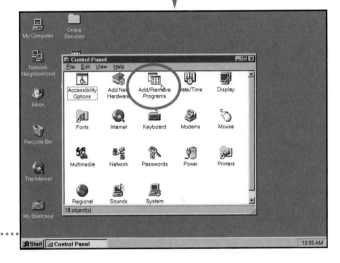

2 In the Control Panel, double-click the **Add/Remove Programs** icon. (Alternatively, select the **Add/Remove Programs** icon and choose **File, Open**.) The Add/Remove Programs Properties dialog box appears.

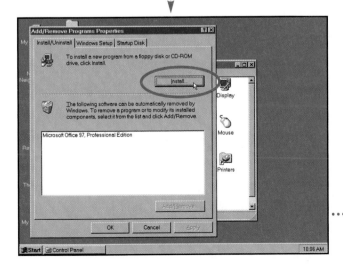

3 In the Install/Uninstall tab, click the **Install** button. The Install Program from Floppy Disk or CD-ROM dialog box appears.

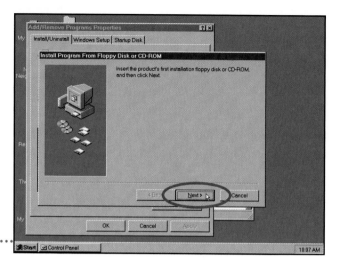

4 Read the instructions, insert the application's first disk or the CD if you haven't already, and choose **Next**.

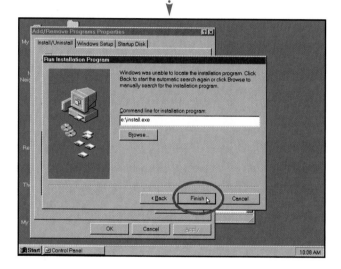

5 Windows finds the file needed to install the program and displays it in the Run Installation Program window. You can choose **Finish** to continue with the installation. You can, alternatively, click the **Browse** command button to look at the disk and choose a different setup or installation file. Choose **Finish**, and Windows installs the program. Answer any questions, change disks, and generally follow the instructions on-screen. ▣

Installing Hardware

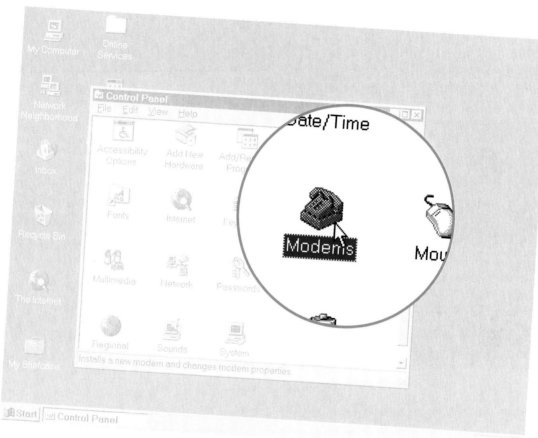

"Why would I do this?"

You can install a new printer, modem, or other hardware quickly and easily by using Windows' wizard feature. Windows guides you to answer questions about the hardware, and if you do not know the answers, Windows can detect the type of hardware and install it with little input from you. Windows calls this handy feature Plug-and-Play. This task shows you how to install a modem.

Task 73: Installing Hardware

1 Connect the modem to your computer. Then open the **Start** menu, choose **Settings,** and choose **Control Panel**. In the Control Panel window, double-click the **Modems** icon. The first wizard dialog box appears.

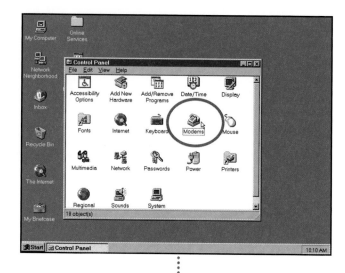

Puzzled?

If you're installing a printer, open the Printer window; if it's a mouse, open the Mouse window. To install controllers, display adapters, sound or video cards, etc., choose the **Add New Hardware** icon.

2 Follow the directions, making a choice to identify the hardware in each Install New Modem dialog box and choosing **Next** when you're ready to move to the next box. (You can choose **Cancel** at any time to stop the process.)

3 When Windows finishes installing the modem, it displays the Modems Properties dialog box listing the device. Click **Finish** to close the dialog box. ■

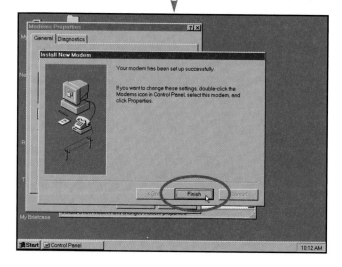

Defragmenting a Disk

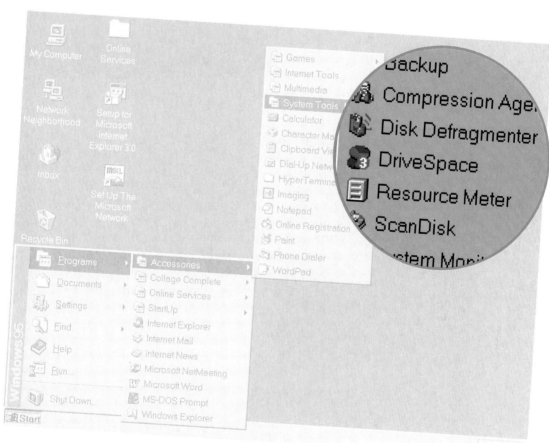

"Why would I do this?"

You can defragment your hard disk to speed access to files and to help prevent potential problems with fragmented files. Defragmenting your disk is a good, general maintenance job you should perform every few months for best results.

Task 74: Defragmenting a Disk

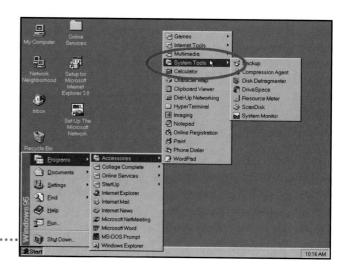

1 Open the **Start** menu and choose **Programs**, **Accessories**, **System Tools**, and finally, **Disk Defragmenter**. The Select Drive dialog box appears.

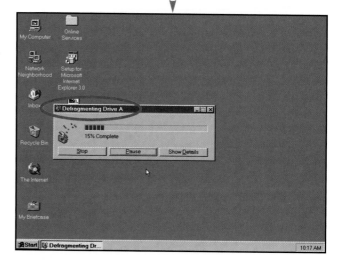

2 You can defragment your hard drive or a disk in a floppy drive. Select the drive you want to defragment from the drop-down list, and then click **OK**. The Defragmenter begins to work.

Missing Link

If the disk does not need to be defragmented, Windows displays a message stating that you can exit or defragment anyway.

3 As the Defragmenter works, its progress appears in the Disk Defragmenter window. You can stop or pause the defragmenting at any time by clicking the appropriate button. When the Defragmenter finishes, a dialog box appears stating that it is done and asking if you want to quit Disk Defragmenter. Choose **Yes** to quit or choose **No** to return to the Select Drive dialog box and defragment another disk. ■

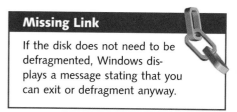

Scanning Your Disk

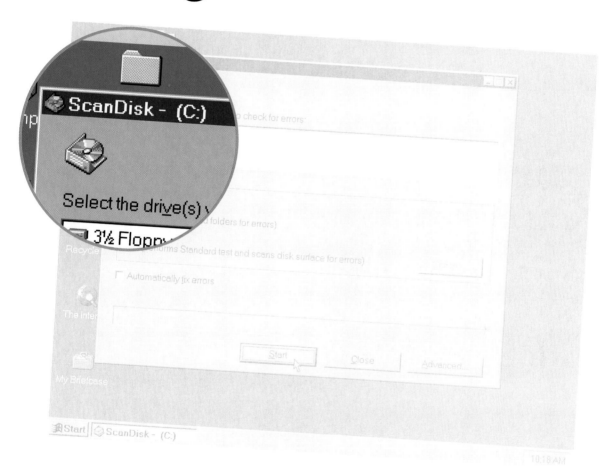

"Why would I do this?"

If you have a damaged disk, Windows may display an error message when you try to open or save a file, or you may notice lost or disarrayed data in some of your files. You can scan the disk for damage using the ScanDisk program and perhaps retrieve the data before you lose it all.

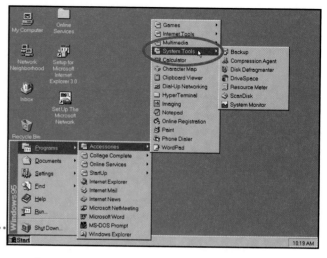

1 Open the **Start** menu and choose **Programs**, **Accessories**, **System Tools**, and **ScanDisk**. The ScanDisk dialog box appears.

2 Choose the drive you want to scan and choose the type of test you want: **Standard** or **Thorough**. Then choose whether you want ScanDisk to automatically fix errors. Click the **Start** button, and ScanDisk scans the selected disk.

Puzzled?

The main difference between the two tests is that the Thorough ScanDisk test methodically checks each sector of the disk in detail, and takes up to four times as long to complete as the Standard. Try Standard first; if it finds problems it cannot fix, then perform the Thorough test.

3 If ScanDisk finds an error, a dialog box appears explaining the error. Read the error message and choose the option that best suits your needs. Click **OK** to continue.

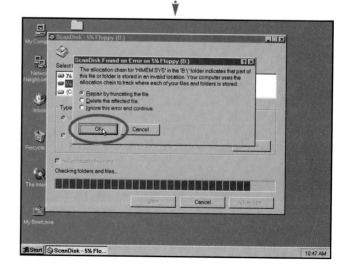

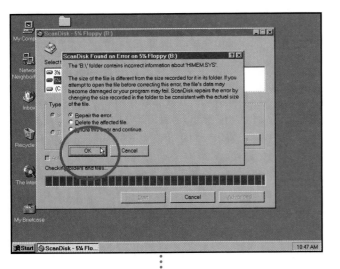

4 Answer any other error messages that appear. If the disk is badly damaged, ScanDisk may not be able to correct the errors. If this happens when you run a standard test, try running the test again and selecting **Thorough**.

Missing Link

If you think a disk might be extremely damaged, try running the Defragmenter on it before you use ScanDisk; this may eliminate some of the errors.

5 When ScanDisk finishes, it displays a report of the scan. Choose **Close** when you're ready to return to the ScanDisk dialog box. Then click the **Close** button to exit ScanDisk. ■

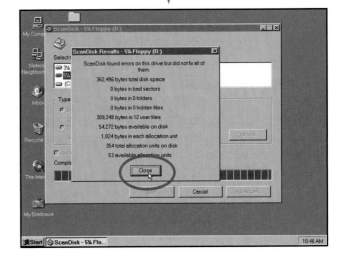

PART XI

References

76 Installing DOS Applications

77 Using the MS-DOS Prompt

78 Using DOS Applications in Windows

ONE ADVANTAGE OF USING WINDOWS is the enormous number of Windows applications available. Various companies produce word processing, database, spreadsheet, drawing, and other programs you can use in Windows. Such a variety of applications provides you with all the tools you need to perform your everyday tasks. In addition to using Windows applications, you can also use DOS applications in Windows.

You're probably most familiar with those DOS applications you've used with previous versions of Windows (3.0, 3.1, or 3.11) or perhaps with a computer running only DOS as its operating system. Some DOS applications you may want to use with Windows 95 include word processors, spreadsheets, games, or accounting programs.

Even though you can successfully install and run DOS programs within Windows 95, I would suggest you upgrade your programs to Windows as soon as possible. Using a Windows program instead of a DOS program with Windows 95 is more efficient and effective—and much less frustrating. However, in case you do need to install and run DOS programs, this part explains how.

When installing DOS applications, you enter a command line in the Run dialog box. The command line, which is found in the application's reference material, includes the drive and file name that installs the Windows application. The drive is a floppy or CD-ROM drive known as A:, B:, D:, or some other such designation. The specified file is an executable file (a file that executes a setup of the application). The executable file, *install.exe* or *setup.exe* for example, is a program that installs files from the floppy disk or CD-ROM to your hard disk. The files it installs are the files that start and operate the new application you are introducing to the computer. Executable files are identified by these common extensions: EXE, PIF, COM, or BAT.

You can install DOS programs using the MS-DOS prompt from Windows. At the DOS prompt, enter the command line specified in the DOS application's documentation, and the program installs. You can then access and use the DOS program at any time through the MS-DOS prompt, which is found in the Programs list in the Start menu.

The biggest advantage of using Windows is the control it gives you over your applications. In Windows 95, you can operate both Windows and DOS applications easily and efficiently. You can even open and use DOS programs (such as WordPerfect for DOS or Lotus 1-2-3 for DOS) within Windows. It is important to realize, however, that opening and using large files from DOS programs within Windows may take extra RAM to work efficiently. *RAM (random-access memory)* is the memory your computer uses to run programs, switch between applications, modify files, and generally carry out procedures as you work. Less RAM causes your system to slow screen redraw, delay file commands such as saving and printing, take longer to access files, and so on. These processes may take even longer when using DOS programs within Windows. Windows recommends that you have 4M to 8M of RAM, preferably 8M if you will be using DOS programs within Windows. In general, the more RAM you have, the more efficiently your computer works.

Installing DOS Applications

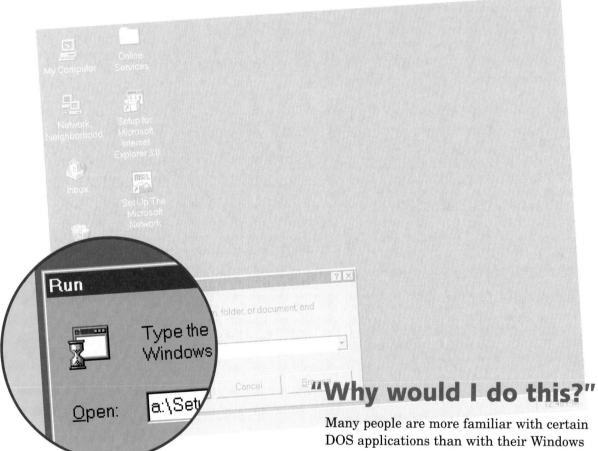

"Why would I do this?"

Many people are more familiar with certain
DOS applications than with their Windows
equivalents and would, therefore, prefer to work
in the DOS applications. Windows enables you
to install DOS applications, such as games,
word processors, and so on, using the Run command. You also can open and use the DOS
applications in Windows, as explained in later
tasks.

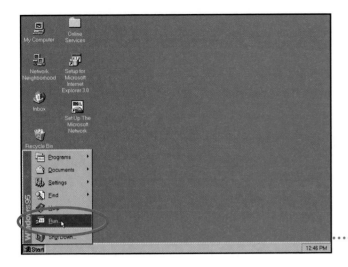

1 Open the **Start** menu and choose the **Run** command. The Run dialog box appears. The Run command enables you to start programs and to install programs.

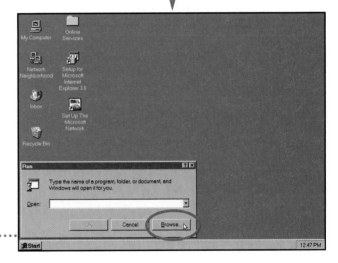

2 In the **Open** text box, enter the letter for the disk drive, followed by the command line needed to install or setup the program (such as **A:\setup**). Skip to step 5. If you do not know the command line, enter the drive letter and a colon (such as **a:**) and then click the **Browse** button.

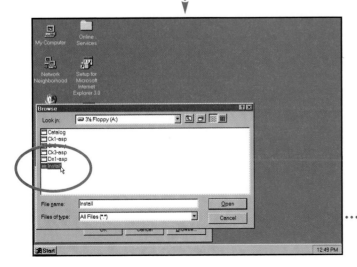

3 The Browse dialog box appears, listing the files on the disk or CD. Select the file called **Install** or **Setup**, and then choose **Open**.

4 The Browse dialog box closes, and Windows returns to the Run dialog box. The Open text box now contains the drive and the install or setup command. Click **OK** to install the program.

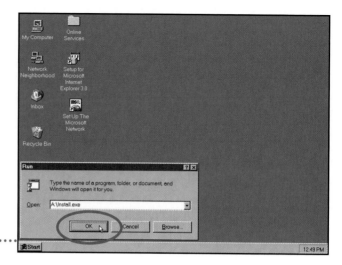

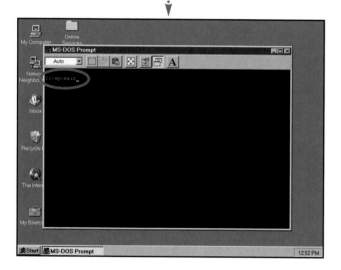

5 Depending on the program you install, Windows may return to the desktop, or it may return to the MS-DOS Prompt window. You can open the application in the MS-DOS window (see Tasks 77 and 78 for more information). To close the MS-DOS Prompt window, type **exit** and press **Enter**. ■

216

Using the MS-DOS Prompt

"Why would I do this?"

There will be times you want to access the DOS prompt from Windows. For example, you might want to run a DOS application or use such DOS commands as MEM, SCANDISK, and so on. For that reason, Windows provides a DOS prompt window you can open while working in Windows.

Task 77: Using the MS-DOS Prompt

1 Open the **Start** menu and select **Pro-grams**. The secondary menu appears. Click **MS-DOS Prompt**, and the DOS window appears with a blinking cursor at the DOS prompt.

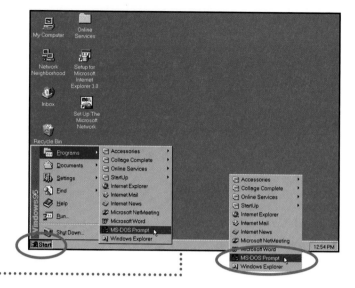

> ### Puzzled?
>
> Your mouse will only work in the DOS Prompt window if you have loaded a mouse driver to DOS. If you want to do that, refer to the documentation that came with your mouse for instructions.

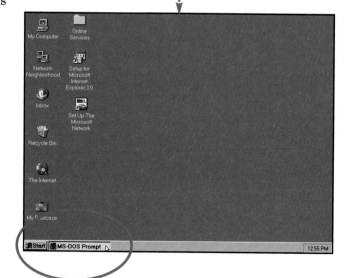

2 Type **cd** and press **Enter** to change to the root directory.

You can run any program by typing the appropriate DOS command. You can also use the icons at the top of the DOS window to mark, copy, paste, enlarge to full screen, set the background, and set the font of the DOS window. The table at the end of this task explains the use of each icon in detail.

3 When you are ready to work with Windows again, click the **Minimize** button on the DOS window. The window is reduced to a button on the taskbar, and you can work in other windows until you need the DOS window again. Click the **MS-DOS Prompt** button on the Windows taskbar at any time to reopen the DOS window.

> ### Puzzled?
>
> Press **Alt+Enter** to enlarge the DOS window to full screen; when you finish, press **Alt+Enter** again to restore the window to its original size.

4 Type **exit** at the DOS prompt and press **Enter** to close the MS-DOS Prompt window. ■

Icon	Description
Auto ▼	Changes the size of the screen and, therefore, the font on-screen.
	Enables you to mark text or a graphic to be copied.
	Creates a copy of any items you have marked with the Mark icon.
	Pastes the copied items in the location of the insertion point.
	Enlarges the MS-DOS Prompt window to fill the entire screen. Press **Alt+Enter** to restore the window's original size.
	Displays the MS-DOS Prompt Properties dialog box.
	Defines whether the program enables background activity, such as background printing.
A	Displays the MS-DOS Prompt Properties dialog box.

Using DOS Applications in Windows

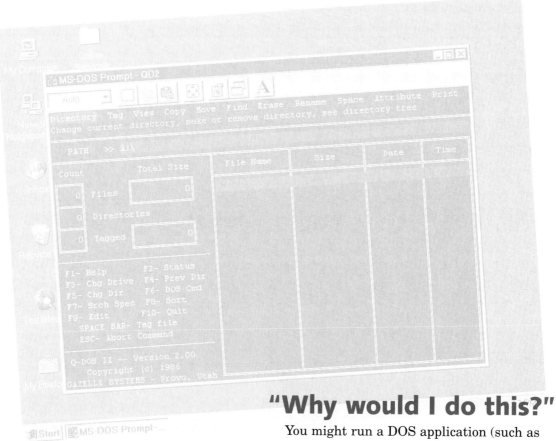

"Why would I do this?"

You might run a DOS application (such as WordPerfect for DOS or Lotus 1-2-3 for DOS) in Windows 95 so that you can work in other Windows 95 applications at the same time. By minimizing the DOS window, you can then open and use other Windows or DOS programs and switch back and forth between the programs you need quickly and easily.

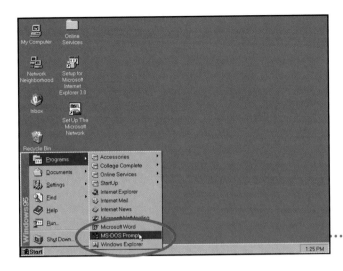

1 Open the **Start** menu, choose **Programs**, and choose **MS-DOS Prompt**. The MS-DOS Prompt window appears.

2 Type **cd** and press **Enter** to move to the root directory, or enter the command required to change to the directory holding the DOS application (such as **cd\qdos** for the QDOS application or **cd\wp60** for WordPerfect for DOS 6.0). Then press **Enter**. At the DOS prompt, enter the name of the program's executable file and press **Enter**; for example, the command **wp** starts the WordPerfect program. The DOS application appears in the DOS window so you can continue your work.

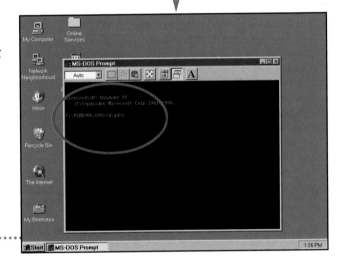

3 When you finish with the DOS application, exit the program as you normally would (choose **File**, **Exit**, or press **F10**, or press **Alt+Q** for example). Windows returns to the DOS prompt. Type **exit** and press **Enter** to close the DOS window. ■

Puzzled?

If the application does not start from the root directory when you enter the name of the program's executable file, you must change to the program's directory.

Index

A

accessing application folders, 64-66
Add Printer Wizard, 120
Add to Address Book command (File menu), 195
adding
    notes to Help topics, 44-45
    printers, 119-122
    shortcuts, 68-69
    Start menu applications, 149
addresses, IP, 187
animation files, 173
Annotate command (Options menu), 45
applications
    closing, 58, 62-63
    data
        copying between, 160-161
        linking between, 164-165
        moving between, 162-163
    DOS
        installing, 214-216
        running in Windows, 220-221
    folders, accessing, 64-66
    opening Windows start up, 131-133
    Paint, 178-181
    RAM, 157
    Start menu
        adding, 149
        starting, 52-53
    starting from files, 54-55
    switching between, 156-157
    tiling, 157
    Windows, installing, 202-204
    WordPad, 174-177

B

background, desktop customizing, 138-139
Browse dialog box, 133
Browse for Folder dialog box, 89

C

Cancel Printing command (Document menu), 115
canceling printing, 114-115
cascading, windows, 20
CD Player, 173
changing
    color schemes, 140-141
    desktop background, 138-139
    display fonts, 151-153
    fonts, WordPad, 176
    mouse settings, 145-147
    printers, settings, 116-118
    Start menu, 148-150
    system date/time, 136-137
    window displays, 17-18
characters, file names, 60, 177
check boxes, 24
choosing printers, 121
clicking, mouse, 3
clipboard
    defined, 81
    viewing, 158-159

Arrange Icons commands (View menu), 96
arranging windows on desktop, 19-20
attaching, e-mail files, 194
Attachments command (File menu), 194
audio files, 173

Clipboard Viewer, installing, 159
Close command (Control menu), 22, 63
Close command (File menu), 22
closing
    applications, 58, 62-63
    windows, 21-22
color schemes, changing, 140-141
colors
    objects, 181
    Paint, 179
commands
    Control menu, Close, 22, 63
    Document menu
        Cancel Printing, 115
        Pause Printing, 115
    Edit menu
        Copy, 81, 98
        Cut, 83, 98
        Paste, 81
        Paste Special, 165
        Undo, 179
    File menu
        Add to Address Book, 195
        Attachments, 194
        Close, 22
        Create Shortcut, 68
        Delete, 87, 100
        Exit, 58
        New, 79, 181
        Pause Printing, 113
        Print, 107
        Print Preview, 107
        Properties, 117
        Restore, 72
        Save, 60
        Save As, 60
        Send Message, 194
        Set As Default, 111
        Update, 167

223

Index

Index

U-V

W-Z

Check out Que® Books on the World Wide Web
http://www.mcp.com/que

As the biggest software release in computer history, Windows 95 continues to redefine the computer industry. Click here for the latest info on our Windows 95 books

Make computing quick and easy with these products designed exclusively for new and casual users

Examine the latest releases in word processing, spreadsheets, operating systems, and suites

The Internet, The World Wide Web, CompuServe®, America Online®, Prodigy® —it's a world of ever-changing information. Don't get left behind!

Find out about new additions to our site, new bestsellers and hot topics

In-depth information on high-end topics: find the best reference books for databases, programming, networking, and client/server technologies

A recent addition to Que, Ziff-Davis Press publishes the highly-successful *How It Works* and *How to Use* series of books, as well as *PC Learning Labs Teaches* and *PC Magazine* series of book/disk packages

Stay on the cutting edge of Macintosh® technologies and visual communications

Find out which titles are making headlines

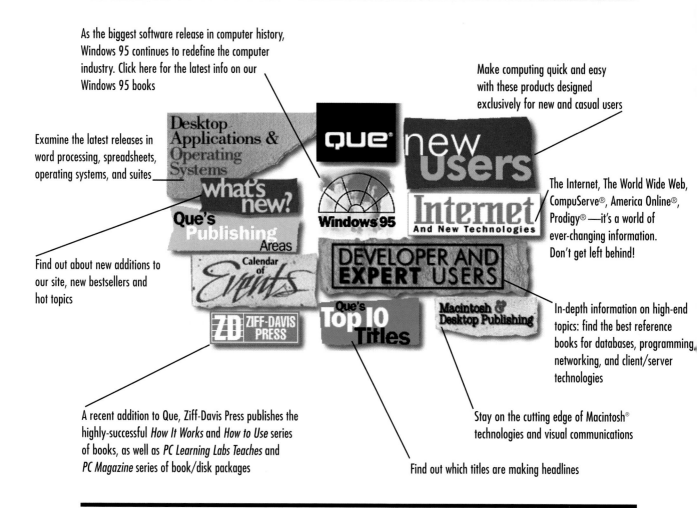

With 6 separate publishing groups, Que develops products for many specific market segments and areas of computer technology. Explore our Web Site and you'll find information on best-selling titles, newly published titles, upcoming products, authors, and much more.

- Stay informed on the latest industry trends and products available
- Visit our online bookstore for the latest information and editions
- Download software from Que's library of the best shareware and freeware

MACMILLAN COMPUTER PUBLISHING USA
A VIACOM COMPANY

Technical ---- Support:

If you need assistance with the information in this book or with a CD/Disk accompanying the book, please access the Knowledge Base on our Web site at **http://www.superlibrary.com/general/support**. Our most Frequently Asked Questions are answered there. If you do not find the answer to your questions on our Web site, you may contact Macmillan Technical Support **(317) 581-3833** or e-mail us at **support@mcp.com**.